Music Therapy with Adults with Learning Disabilities

Edited by Tessa Watson

Routledge
Taylor & Francis Group
OCM 77520589
LONDON AND NEW YORK

First published 2007
by Routledge
27 Church Road, Hove, East Sussex BN3 2FA

Simultaneously published in the USA and Canada
by Routledge
270 Madison Avenue, New York, NY 10016

Routledge is an imprint of the Taylor & Francis Group, an informa business

Typeset in Times by Garfield Morgan, Swansea, West Glamorgan
Printed and bound in Great Britain by TJ International Ltd, Padstow, Cornwall
Paperback cover design by Gavin Ambrose

British Library Cataloguing in Publication Data
A catalogue record for this book is available from the British Library

Library of Congress Cataloging-in-Publication Data
Music therapy with adults with learning difficulties / edited by Tessa Watson.
    p. cm.
  Includes bibliographical references and index.
  ISBN 978-0-415-37908-3 (hardback) – ISBN 978-0-415-37909-0
(paperback) 1. Music therapy. 2. Learning disabilities–Treatment. 3. Learning
disabled–Rehabilitation. I. Watson, Tessa, 1967–
  ML3920.M89965 2007
615.8'5154–dc22

                                                         2006102044

ISBN: 978-0-415-37908-3 (hbk)
ISBN: 978-0-415-37909-0 (pbk)

Music Therapy with Adults with Learning Disabilities

Music Therapy with Adults with Learning Disabilities explores how music therapists work in partnership with people with learning disabilities to encourage independence and empowerment, and to address a wide variety of everyday issues and difficulties.

Comprehensive and wide-ranging, this book describes in detail the role and work of the music therapist with adults with learning disabilities. Many clinical examples are used, including casework with people with autism, Asperger's syndrome, profound and multiple learning disabilities and a dual diagnosis of learning disability and mental health problems. The book also explores issues of teamwork and collaborative working, considering how music therapists and their colleagues can best work together. The chapters are grouped into four sections: an introduction to current music therapy work and policy in the area, clinical work with individuals, clinical work with groups, and collaborative and teamwork. Guidelines for good practice are also provided.

This is a thought-provoking and topical text for all those involved in work with adults with learning disabilities. It is essential reading for music therapists and fellow professionals, carers, policymakers and students.

Tessa Watson is a music therapist and music therapy trainer. She is convenor of the music therapy training course at Roehampton University. Tessa's current clinical work is with adults with learning disabilities for Ealing Primary Care Trust where she is Principal Arts Therapist.

Contents

Contributors   vii

Foreword   ix
TONY WIGRAM

Acknowledgements   xii

Introduction   1
TESSA WATSON

1   Valuing people: a new framework   5
    TESSA WATSON

2   Music therapy with adults with learning disabilities:
    sharing stories   18
    TESSA WATSON

3   Music therapy and autistic spectrum disorder   33
    RHIAN SAVILLE

4   Challenging behaviour: working with the blindingly obvious   47
    CATHY WARNER

5   'What bit of my head is talking now?': music therapy with
    people with learning disabilities and mental illness   58
    ELEANOR RICHARDS

6   Friendship and group work   71
    CLARE L. FILLINGHAM

7   Community, culture and group work   85
    TESSA WATSON

 8 Working with people with profound and multiple learning
    disabilities in music therapy   98
    TESSA WATSON

 9 Looking in from the outside: communicating effectively
    about music therapy work   112
    BEN SAUL

10 Multidisciplinary working and collaborative working in
    music therapy   121
    KAREN TWYFORD AND TESSA WATSON

    Appendix I: Guidelines for good practice for music therapists   133
    Appendix II: Useful organizations and websites   137
    References   140
    Index   157

Contributors

Tessa Watson is a music therapist and music therapy trainer. She is convenor of the music therapy training course at Roehampton University. She has worked with a variety of client groups in mental health and learning disabilities, her current clinical work being with adults with learning disabilities for Ealing Primary Care Trust. Tessa has undertaken research in learning and teaching in the arts therapies, music therapy work with adults with learning disabilities, and women in secure psychiatric services, and regularly speaks about and publishes her work.

Rhian Saville trained as a music therapist at the Guildhall School of Music and Drama and is currently Head Music Therapist at Nottingham Healthcare NHS Trust. She has worked with children and adults in learning disability and mental health for 13 years, having a particular interest in people with autism.

Cathy Warner PhD is senior lecturer in music therapy at the University of the West of England. She has 13 years of clinical experience in the fields of learning disability, mental health, bereavement and neurology, and has presented and published her work widely. She is particularly interested in the perspective of the client within music therapy research.

Eleanor Richards is Senior Lecturer in Music Therapy at Anglia Ruskin University, Cambridge, and Senior Music Therapist at Cambridgeshire and Peterborough Mental Health Partnership NHS Trust, where she works with adults with learning disabilities. Also a psychotherapist in private practice, she has a particular interest in the applications of attachment theory to therapeutic work with people with learning disabilities. She is the author of a range of articles and papers, and co-editor of *Music Therapy and Group Work*.

Clare L. Fillingham is Lead Music Therapist for NHS Borders in Scotland, covering adult learning disability and mental health. She trained at Guildhall School of Music and completed a Masters research degree at University of Roehampton in 2003. She is currently completing a training in group analytic psychotherapy in Glasgow.

Ben Saul works with adults with learning disabilities and challenging behaviour in Greenwich and is part of the transdisciplinary assessment team based at the Greenwich PCT Child Development Centre. He runs introductory courses on music therapy at City University, London.

Karen Twyford trained as a music therapist at the University of Melbourne, Australia. She has worked primarily in the area of special education in the UK and Australia. Her recent masters research investigated the use of collaborative multidisciplinary approaches amongst music therapists and other professionals in the United Kingdom.

Foreword

Tony Wigram

Music Therapy with Adults with Learning Disabilities is a very welcome addition to the literature, especially because this population has attracted much less attention in the past compared with other populations. The impact of a learning disability is most keenly felt when an increasing lack of services and support fails to recognise the uniqueness and potentials of this group within our society. In a world where labels carry more and more weight, paradoxically because of the label 'learning disability' we are all frequently guilty of underestimating and consequently reducing our expectations of people with mild, moderate, severe or profound learning disabilities. This fascinating book opens a door into a creative world, allowing us to be both reassured and challenged, and to realise what music used therapeutically can mean.

Tessa Watson has brought together an experienced and highly skilled group of contributors to offer a detailed exploration and understanding of the value of music therapy in this multifaceted area. The book offers insights into the role of music therapy in addressing the real and everyday issues that people with learning disability face – the need to be recognised, listened to, understood and to open up their emotions through a medium that allows anger as much as happiness, sadness as well as joy, and bewilderment, fear and anxiety. Expressing difficult, sometimes painful emotions is not negative; it is as necessary and healthy as positive emotional experiences. We frequently discuss whether therapies meet health needs – well having someone listen and respond to your frustration and anger is also a health need, and as much a healthy process as physical treatments.

Tessa Watson sets the scene by offering a practical and focused explanation of the relevance and scope of music therapy, illustrating this through the process of three imagined people. This opening section provides such a useful understanding from referral to therapy, valuable for many differing groups – trainee music therapists, music therapy clinicians and educators from within the profession, and disciplines within the multidisciplinary team and managers of services from without. Tessa Watson also addresses the need to connect clinical practice with theory – and the support of cited literature pervades all chapters of this book.

The second section delves into three subgroups with diagnoses of autism (Rhian Saville), challenging behaviour (Cathy Warner) and people with dual diagnoses (Eleanor Richards). People with these specific problems have been referred for music therapy since first reports of the beneficial therapeutic effects of music were documented. All three contributors describe very well the focus of the work, but I was (as usual) particularly impressed with the case examples which do so much to bring alive the discussion. Social engagement, self-understanding and a preparedness to engage in deep emotional contact is the way these contributors explicate the importance of music therapy, at the same time illustrating the expertise of the therapist.

My own abiding memories from 21 years of working in a large institution for adults and children with learning disabilities is the group work, and it is very welcome to find in this book three important chapters documenting group music therapy. Clare Fillingham's case example shows us how well music therapy facilitates group dynamics and relationships, and the included research study, looking at perceptions of friendships and how they developed over time (pre/post results) between group members demonstrates very 'client-centred' research. Tessa Watson's chapter shows how clearly she has centred her work within the culture and community of her clients, and their needs from the community. I personally resonated with her chapter on music therapy with people with profound and multiple learning disability, which was in fact the clinical population with whom I took my first faltering steps as a newly qualified music therapist many years ago. Music therapy's style of work through empathic engagement at the person's level is really evident in Tessa Watson's work, as well as a recognition of the need for some structure in group work. Nind and Hewitt's original work into intensive interaction emerged when they came to join the teams at my own institution in the 1980s, and was (I am sure) clearly influenced by seeing the music therapy approach of working at the client's level, as indeed we were later influenced by the highly skilled methods they developed. Tessa Watson illustrates with detail the influence of musical elements – particularly melody, harmony and the importance of singing.

I also welcome the attention given to effectively communicating about music therapy to the wider audience, and this theme is addressed by Ben Saul, Karen Twyford and Tessa Watson. The significance of recognising music therapy as a therapy, and how others might perceive and understand this work in the lives of the people is well discussed. The dialogue between members of a multidisciplinary team is informative, insightful, and reflects recognition of the work by other professionals, not to mention the impact a group improvisation and workshops had had on this team.

There is so much in this book, and the integrating influence of Tessa Watson is evident. Contributing four of the ten chapters herself, and one co-authored, Tessa Watson has provided music therapists, related professionals, carers, parents and professionals with a wonderful insight into the importance of music therapy for people with learning disabilities. This book is essential reading for all students of music therapy, and for clinicians. Music therapy for adults with learning disabilities is well resourced, guiding, inspiring, and helps us to understand why people with learning disabilities find music therapy so relevant for them.

Acknowledgements

Tessa Watson would like to acknowledge the constant support and encouragement of Peter Hutchison. She would also like to thank colleagues for their interest in the book, in particular the staff at Stirling Road and Carlton Road Day Centres for their support for music therapy.

Introduction

Tessa Watson

Prologue

In a room in the community centre, six people sit, clients and music therapists, playing instruments and singing together. Maggie is kicking a drum with her foot, making a loud sound. She hears one of the music therapists respond on the violin, laughs and begins to sing. At this moment she is the soloist in this piece of group music, engaged in a close dialogue with others, controlling what happens next, making choices and influencing the music. Her expressive vocal sounds seem to carry feelings of both joy and pain. When the music ends, there is a satisfied silence and no need for words. Maggie has profound and multiple learning disabilities and needs help with all aspects of her daily life. Her experience in music therapy helps her to relate beyond these disabilities, achieve self-expression and engage in profoundly satisfying relationships.

Later in the day, Nick ends his session by coming close to the music therapist, looking her in the eyes and telling her, 'I liked music therapy today.' He has been in the room for his usual 40-minute session. In other settings he finds it hard to spend more than five minutes with another person or to look at someone's face. Nick uses the sessions to expressively play the instruments with the therapist, talk and think, and sometimes write song lyrics which reflect upon his life experiences. Nick has found it useful to use the instruments to show how angry he can feel. He is able to express his strong feelings without damaging the therapeutic relationship that allows him to share, process and reflect upon these experiences. Nick has learning disabilities, autism and additional mental health problems, and finds much of life confusing and frightening.

The themes of the book

Music Therapy with Adults with Learning Disabilities is the first book to focus entirely on this important work undertaken with clients with a variety of diagnoses of learning disability. It gives an insight both into music therapy work, and the issues faced by people with learning disabilities in their lives, illustrated by many case examples of music therapy clinical work. Most music therapy work is undertaken in a confidential therapeutic setting. However, music therapists need to find ways to share information about their work. This book provides a detailed picture of that work which will be of interest not only to music therapists but also to others interested in finding out about the profession or work within this area.

A learning disability is a diagnosis of significant intellectual impairment and deficits in basic everyday skills, present from childhood (Emerson *et al.* 2001). Surveys indicate that at present over one million adults in the UK have a mild or severe learning disability. Having a learning disability has a different impact for each person due to the wide range of different diagnoses and difficulties that are encompassed in the term. These diagnoses are described within the chapters of this book, and consideration is given to the impact that the varying conditions might have for a fulfilling life. People with learning disabilities have been marginalized and often badly treated throughout history, and are only now being encouraged to find their own voices and take a full place in society and community. As Arthur states: 'the emotional lives and emotional difficulties of people with learning disabilities have been largely neglected' (2003: 25). This book explores how music therapists work in partnership with people with learning disabilities in the area of relationships and emotions, encouraging independence and empowerment, and addressing a wide variety of issues and difficulties.

Music therapy is a primarily non-verbal form of therapeutic intervention, making it particularly suitable for people who have communication difficulties or who find it hard to talk about their feelings. People who have difficulties interacting with others, or who use behaviour that challenges can also find this therapy to be an accessible approach. John states that music therapy can be viewed as 'experience oriented rather than insight oriented' (John 1995: 160), allowing people to have an experience of finding different ways of being with others, of expressing and sharing their feelings and of telling their stories through music, when words are not available. Music therapy therefore has great relevance for this client group due to the accessibility of the non-verbal medium of music and the opportunities it gives for forming relationships, and sharing and expressing feelings. The different chapters in the book explore the whole range of clinical work in this area: from individual and group work, to collaborative work with other professionals where knowledge and skills are shared.

Music therapists in the United Kingdom have worked with adults with learning disabilities since the 1960s, and yet the work has been infrequently documented. Aware of this gap in the music therapy literature, I began to think of bringing together the first book that would document experiences in music therapy with adults with learning disabilities in order to describe and validate relationships and work that I have found both profound and moving. All those contributing to this book have encountered people who have displayed resilience and strength, who have worked hard in their therapy and have much to teach us about life and disability.

In the past few years there has been more dialogue between music therapists working with adults with learning disabilities, perhaps because of the need to address issues raised by government policy and legislation. It seems timely to invite other authors to share their work and recent research. These authors have brought energy and enthusiasm to the task of documenting their clinical work and research, and have made it a pleasure to edit this book.

Those reading the book will probably be aware that the government has focused on the area of learning disability in recent years, with the publication of the White Paper *Valuing People* in 2001, and this has had a significant impact on the way in which learning disability services are delivered (DOH 2001c). The themes and questions that this book raises and addresses are therefore timely. The aim of *Valuing People* was to improve the life chances of people with learning disabilities, focusing on the principles of rights, independence, choice and inclusion. This book explores in detail the way in which these issues are central to music therapy work, and how music therapists address these themes (see Chapter 1). These developments are relevant not only to work in the UK but internationally, in terms of the movement towards advocacy, independence and fulfilling lives.

The structure of the book

The book divides into four sections. The first part comprises two chapters that give a detailed history and overview of the areas of learning disability and music therapy. Chapter 1 provides information about what a learning disability is and how it impacts on lives, families and communities. A summary of the history of this population is given, concluding with an outline of recent thinking and policymaking. The history of music therapy within this clinical area is then considered, including a literature review. Chapter 2 looks in detail at the work of the music therapist, asking the question: what happens in the therapy room? The work is brought to life as we meet and follow three imagined clients in their progress through therapy. Throughout the chapter there are points of reflection on theory and practice, giving a comprehensive picture of music therapy work.

The second part of the book is concerned with work with individuals with specific diagnoses. The authors give information about each diagnosis and the way in which it might affect a person's life, an overview of music therapy approaches and strategies, and illustrate their writing with clinical examples. Rhian Saville considers autism and Asperger's syndrome, summarizing recent theoretical debate and describing a case study of work with a young man undertaken over four years. Cathy Warner writes about challenging behaviour, presenting the main issues in this difficult area of work and describing a clinical case study that considers the work of four individuals within a group. Eleanor Richards discusses the issues for clients with a dual diagnosis of learning disability and mental health problems.

The third part of the book describes group work. In Chapter 6, Clare Fillingham looks at group work and friendship, giving an overview of group work theories and using her recent research to illustrate the way in which music therapy can contribute towards widening social networks. My own work is then documented in two further chapters, first Chapter 7 about music therapy and community work. This chapter outlines concepts of community, including recent theoretical developments in music therapy, and describes group work specifically set up to address issues around community life. Chapter 8 is concerned with work with people with profound and multiple learning disabilities. An overview of the issues for these clients is given and illustrated with a case study of a group.

The last part of the book is concerned with the issue of teamwork. In Chapter 9, Ben Saul considers how the outside world views music therapy, using recent research to show how carers consider that music therapy can help clients, and what this means for music therapy practitioners. In Chapter 10 Karen Twyford and I consider the concepts of multidisciplinary and collaborative working in music therapy, outlining these concepts, presenting a discussion between multidisciplinary colleagues, and illustrating these ideas with examples of collaborative work between colleagues. Appendix I gives good practice guidelines for music therapy clinicians and Appendix II lists useful organizations and websites.

A note on terminology

I have chosen to use the term learning disability throughout the book, as this is the terminology that I am familiar with in my work in the NHS. However, I am aware that some people prefer the term learning difficulty, and I hope that the reader will imagine that these are interchangeable. The terms client and service user are used at different points throughout the book by different authors, illustrating differences in the use of words and terminology. These issues of terminology are considered in Chapter 1.

In conclusion, it is hoped that this book will be a thought-provoking read and provide knowledge and guidance to music therapists, fellow professionals and carers and others interested in this area of work.

Valuing people

A new framework

Tessa Watson

A history of learning disabilities

The first part of this chapter looks at what a learning disability is and how it affects everyday life. Knowing about these facts and their consequences helps workers to be aware of important issues that might arise during clinical work.

Definitions and causes of learning disability

The definition of a learning disability includes the presence of:

- a significant intellectual impairment
- deficits in social functioning or adaptive behaviour (basic everyday skills) which are present from childhood (Emerson *et al.* 2001).

In order to ascertain that a person has a significant intellectual impairment, it is usual to refer to intelligence quotient (IQ). An IQ of below 70 is the current score used to indicate a learning disability (measured with the Wechler Adult Intelligence Scale). The World Health Organization International Classification of Diseases (WHO 1992) details four categories of IQ: mild, moderate, severe and profound. It is arguable that these are neither accurate nor useful, due to both the difficulty and value of assessing disability in this way. The interaction between the person and their environment is now considered as important as IQ in assessing disability. Living and working in a familiar, predictable environment will lead someone to have greater coping skills than if they were in an unfamiliar environment with few cues or communication aids.

Causes of learning disability are not always clear, and because of this some people may not have a specific diagnosis. It is accepted that biological, environmental and social factors are all involved in the aetiology of a learning disability. Recent research suggests that in the case of those with a mild learning disability there is often an association with social class and unstable family background. Readers are referred to Emerson *et al.* (2001) which gives a comprehensive explanation of the different diagnoses of learning disability. Biological factors that can cause a learning disability can be summarized as being genetic (chromosome or gene disorders), antenatal (damage during pregnancy such as infections, intoxication and physical damage), perinatal (damage during birth) and postnatal (damage after birth such as infections or injury). The most commonly known diagnoses are Down's syndrome, fragile X syndrome and autistic spectrum disorder (ASD, which includes autism and Asperger's syndrome). It is estimated that in the UK there are between 580,000 and 1,750,000 people with a mild learning disability and 230,000–350,000 with a severe learning disability. Many people with a mild disability do not use specialist services.

Most people with learning disabilities have some form of communication difficulty, which in its turn may cause emotional and behavioural difficulties. About half of these people also have a sensory impairment such as vision or hearing loss, and many have an additional physical disability. Some people may use behaviour which challenges and this is often considered as a response to a situation or experience. In addition to their primary disability, this population may be more likely to experience other health problems such as epilepsy (approximately 30 per cent).

People with learning disabilities who experience difficult or adverse life events may also experience a mental health problem (approximately 40 per cent, including episodes of depression, anxiety, self-injury, or more enduring illnesses such as schizophrenia and bipolar affective disorder). Sinason (1992) describes the burden of handicap as depleting the resources of the individual, making a mental health problem more likely.

Social history

Much has been written about the history of this population (Alaszewski 1988; Brown and Smith 1992; Dumbleton 1998; Malin 1987; Race 1995; Thomas and Woods 2003; Walmsley and Ralph 2002), and this is now summarized briefly. Called 'fools' or 'natural fools', people with learning disabilities were accepted as part of society until the 1600s. With the Age of Enlightenment came clearer ideas about power, education and employability, and having a learning disability became a stigma and often meant life in the workhouse. The first laws and policies in this area are observed in the Victorian era (e.g. the Mental Deficiency Act 1913), when the morality of the time encouraged harsh treatment and a negative, judging attitude. The ideas behind institutions of the time were broadly based in education, but there was much ill-treatment and poor conditions. Individuals were segregated from their communities and men and women were not allowed to mix. Later, as eugenics became a popular idea, families were blamed for producing a child with disabilities. People with learning disabilities were considered to have a negative influence on those around them, and as a result led limited, regimented lives. We gain an insight into the extremes of thinking of this time from Tredgold's statement: 'It would be an economical and humane procedure were their existence to be painlessly terminated' (cited in Race 2002: 33).

Sinason articulates the issues of euphemism that arise for a population who have been negatively labelled. She traces the history of terms from blockhead, cretin, imbecile, retard, subnormal to disability and reminds us:

> Nearly every book on mental handicap written in the last hundred years begins with a chapter on definitions and words chosen. Each such chapter praises itself for its hopeful new term. It is therefore doing a grave disservice to past pioneers to point contemptuously to their chosen terms. Within another five years the process of euphemism will already be affecting the brave new words.
>
> (Sinason 1992: 40)

With the inception of the welfare state and National Health Service (NHS) in 1948, asylums became hospitals and people with learning disabilities began to be cared for by health professionals. Race notes that with this era began the 'clear footprint of the medical model' (2002: 36). However, there was no specific training for the work and it was not popular. Gradual change occurred as theorists began to suggest that a hospital should be a place of development and rehabilitation. In 1964 Jack Tizard began his pioneering work, writing about the need for better services. At this time most people with learning disabilities were living in large hospitals, alienated and excluded from society, with little control over their lives. For many, this was their whole life experience. David Barron (a patient) illustrates this, stating: 'It was an awful life inside the hospital although I knew no other way of living' (Barron 1989).

Gradually, in the 1960s and 1970s, the concept of normalization began to change services, and the writing of Wolfensberger was brought to the UK from Denmark and the USA (normalization was renamed social role valorization in 1983 to focus attention on the need for valued social roles for people with learning disabilities). As thinking changed, the theme of deinstitutionalization became important. In the UK, the governmental Jay report (HMSO 1979) laid down several principles which valued inclusion in society. O'Brien wrote on 'the principles of ordinary life' (1987), and developed accomplishments by which services could measure their achievements.

In 1990 the Community Care Act began the process of closing hospitals and resettling residents into the community (DOH 1990). The numbers of people living in hospital decreased from 51,000 in 1976 to 3638 in 2002

(Emerson 2004; O'Hara and Sperlinger 1997). Most people with learning disabilities now live in residential services in the community. This has brought them many positive benefits including a greater quality of life, individual support and inclusion in community and society. In parallel with these changes in thinking and delivery of services, terminology changed first to mental handicap and then learning disability (the term chosen by the Department of Health in 1990), or learning difficulty (the term preferred by some service users). Alongside these developments, the idea of a social model of disability was growing. This model encourages a socially aware, inclusive culture, and brings attention to the barriers to full living faced by people with disabilities.

Current frameworks for practice

This part of the chapter will summarize recent NHS and government guidance, including the 2001 government White Paper, *Valuing People* (DOH 2001c). Since the 1990s there has been an increase in literature, training and initiatives developing values of advocacy, partnership, inclusion and person-centred services. As the idea of partnership began to develop between agencies, different models of disability such as social and medical models were compared, leading to a more holistic approach.

The DOH publication *Signposts for Success* promoted physical health and therapeutic interventions, stating that services should ensure that people with learning disabilities had opportunities to 'lead a life which promotes mental health and well-being, including communication, relationship building, busy and interesting days and personal achievement' (1998: 9) and 'develop and learn throughout their lives by encouraging independence, self-determination and planned risk taking as an aid to personal growth and learning' (p. 9).

Also in 1998, the *Human Rights Act* was published, giving the right for all people to a family life, and the right to education (HMSO 1998). These two rights directly link with independence and self-determination, and therefore have an impact on what is considered possible for people with learning disabilities. In 2001 the government White Paper *Valuing People* was published (DOH 2001c). In 2005 two pieces of guidance were published: first, the *Mental Capacity Act* which outlined a statutory framework aiming to empower and protect vulnerable people who are not able to make their own decisions (DOH 2005a); second, a government paper titled *Improving the Life Chances of Disabled People* which aimed to ensure that 'disabled people should have full opportunities and chances to improve their quality of life . . . as equal members of society' (Cabinet Office 2005: 1). In 2006 the government White Paper *Our Health, Our Care, Our Say* set out plans for the development of health and social care services in the community (DOH 2006).

Thus recent thinking and policymaking allow us to work with clients within a framework that values their contributions and encourages a vision of more fulfilling futures. *Valuing People*, and the Scottish equivalent *The Same as You* (Scottish Executive 2001), were broadly welcomed as giving a comprehensive vision for work with this client group in the twenty-first century (see critiques in Eliatamby and Hampton 2001; McGill 2005; Williams 2005). In these publications, principles and strategies for work with people with learning disabilities are given, and issues in their lives considered. Many of the developments of previous decades are taken forward, and at its heart are four main principles: rights, independence, choice and inclusion (DOH 2001c). A summary of these issues is given below.

Working together

Recent writing implies that efficient communication and exchange of information between workers and across organizational boundaries (health, social services, independent and charity organizations) provides more effective services. In particular, health and social services workers now form joint teams, sharing client care. This places importance on strong multi-disciplinary and multi-agency working and gives a responsibility to the music therapist, along with other workers, to find appropriate and efficient ways of communicating (with due consideration to confidentiality) about their work. This may be with individual workers concerning particular clients, or through contribution to planning or professionals meetings. Communication systems should also allow contact with partner organizations such as voluntary organizations, schools or mental health service providers. In addition, training may be provided for colleagues about the role of the music therapist within a team or organization. Race (2002) considers that this helps to provide consistency of values between workers and services.

Contact with the client's family can be useful for all involved, allowing discussion of key issues as the person progresses in their therapy. However, when working with adult clients with learning disabilities it can be unclear how much contact with parents or other family members might be appropriate. Music therapists might hold review meetings with the client and invited members of the family. The content of the meeting could be negotiated with the client, who may wish to lead part or all of the meeting, in order to maintain a sense of control.

Advocacy and person-centred planning

Valuing People states that 'it is no longer acceptable for organisations to view people with learning disabilities as passive recipients of services; they must instead be seen as active partners' (DOH 2001c: 51). Great importance is now placed on a culture of self-advocacy, advocacy or empowerment, in order that clients can have a voice and control over their lives. Advocacy can be described as speaking up, or speaking on behalf of a person about a particular issue (Aspis 2002). Empowerment is the process of enabling people to take control of their own lives. Advocacy groups and user forums contribute greatly to an understanding of the needs and wishes of people with learning disabilities.

As part of this culture of advocacy, the concept of person-centred planning (PCP) is articulated. PCP is described by Towell as 'a way of assisting people to work out what they want, the support they require and helping them get it' (2004: 12). PCP encourages clients to think, with appropriate people, about their lives, dreams and aspirations, and to develop plans for the future. The idea of following the lead of the client through a person-centred process is familiar to the music therapist who may be invited to contribute to a PCP or planning circle because of the close and reciprocal contact that has been established with the person involved.

Accessible information is frequently used when working in a person-centred way, and a PCP record might include accessible signs and symbols, such as Makaton (a communication system adapted from British Sign Language), photographs, videotape or a computer program as a way of documenting the client's opinions and personality. Music therapists might also use accessible information in their work: to communicate dates and times as well as breaks in therapy, or to help a client to identify or articulate a particular emotion or experience. Accessible information could be used in relation to paperwork such as referral forms, information sheets or reports (see Grove *et al.* 2000).

Healthy lifestyles

Health professionals have a responsibility to promote good health and healthy lifestyles. At first sight it might be thought that it is not part of the role of a music therapist to directly address issues relating to a healthy lifestyle. Music therapy work is most closely linked to promoting healthy lifestyles in the areas of communication, mental health, independence and skills, sexuality and relationships and challenging needs. Embedded within this is the promotion of good emotional and mental health, and greater independence and skills in these areas.

In order to promote healthy lifestyles, NHS settings have been directed by the Department of Health to provide each client with a health action plan (HAP). This is defined as 'a personal plan about what a person with learning disabilities can do to be healthy'. HAPs and health facilitation are 'about supporting good emotional health as well as good physical health. So this is about your feelings as well as your body' (DOH 2002: 4). Currently, the emphasis of health action plans tends to be on physical health.

However, mental health should also be considered and protocols are to be developed between mental health and learning disability services.

Culturally appropriate services

Mir *et al.* (2001: 13) remind us that 'the personal and collective values and experiences of people within minority groups are often different from those of the majority population' (see also Nadirshaw 1997). Minority ethnic communities face some inequalities and discrimination in employment, education, health and social services, and there is a higher prevalence of learning disability in South Asian communities. There are different ways of thinking about disability and workers may need to explore the attitudes and beliefs of the client and their family in order to be able to work sensitively with issues brought to therapy. For example, there may be cultural expectations about the role of a person with a learning disability in the family, or about what they can achieve, along with expectations of the roles of family carers.

Transition

Transitions from school to college, to a day centre or job, and in old age are important times of change. In reality they cannot always be planned, and clients and their families can find periods of transition unsettling or distressing. The emotional impact of leaving school, which may have provided a positive structure and progression through childhood years, can be significant, as young adults confront the reality that they may not have their dream job or go to university like their siblings. Whilst for many, leaving school is the start of a career or further study and an exciting introduction to independence, young adults with learning disabilities are often confronted with little choice or structure. There may be too few places on appropriate courses at college or further education, or only a couple of days available at a day centre. *Valuing People* stresses the need for services to work together to 'ensure effective links are in place within and between children's and adult's service in both health and social services' (DOH 2001c: 43).

Other transitions that mark the beginning of a fully independent, adult life are gaining employment and leaving home. For people with learning disabilities, leaving home may not happen in a natural, positive way, but during a time of crisis (for example, when a parent dies). Employment, one of the ways in which we gain a sense of identity, self-worth, and also a place where many relationships are made, is an important part of adult life. There are now more job opportunities available for people with learning disabilities, some within supportive schemes (Mencap 2002). Towards the end of life, Walker and Walker (2002) consider some of the issues around independence for people with learning disabilities who are ageing.

External realities and internal worlds

Fulfilling lives are experienced in both practical and emotional terms. Adults with learning disabilities may be struggling actively or passively (consciously or unconsciously), with the emotional impact of their disability and the obstacles that it raises to interacting in an easy, normal way. Hodges talks about 'painful external realities and painful internal worlds' that may be experienced due both to disability and the world's response to these (2003). In 2005 Emerson *et al.* found that only 47 per cent of those people with learning disabilities they interviewed were 'very happy' with their lives.

People with learning disabilities might need different kinds of help in order to use both their personal resources and the opportunities open to them. An idealistic stance may find professionals taking polarized positions, as Skelly describes: '"you are denying this person choice" versus "you are denying this person's difficulties"' (2002: 42). Reyes-Simpson suggests that 'the drive for "normalisation" often rides rough-shod over the child's or adult's actual needs' (2004: 125). These authors' writing echoes Wolfensberger's (1983) statement:

> Unpleasant realities are apt to be denied and repressed into unconsciousness, especially if they stand in contrast to the higher values and ideals that people consciously profess. Such denial and repression can take place on a systemic (e.g. societal or organisational) level as well as on a personal/individual one. . . . Normalisation incorporates the explicit assumption that consciousness is preferable to unconsciousness and that negative feelings and dynamics should and usually have to be made conscious in order to be adaptively addressed.
>
> (cited in Brown and Smith 1992: 85)

The implementation of modern strategies may, paradoxically, pose challenges for some people with learning disabilities, who need additional support in order to access their communities and take up opportunities for more independent, fulfilling lives. It is daunting to be part of a world that is curious and sometimes discriminatory or cruel. Making sense of a busy community environment, and in particular managing positive contact with others, presents major hurdles. Some people may need an environment such as music therapy to help them think about these new challenges, and what they want or do not want from these new experiences.

In order to work with people with learning disabilities to enable them to have full lives, greater access to their communities and to allow them to fulfil their dreams and wishes, it is sometimes necessary to offer specialist help. In the publication *Include Us Too*, people with learning disabilities state that emotional and mental health, and friendships and relationships are two key areas for services to address (Community Care Development

Centre 2002). Bayley (1997a, 1997b) details the different qualities that we all need in our relationships in order to give us self-esteem and a sense of being valued. These include belonging and attachment, social integration, reassurance of worth and exercise of choice (see also Ourvry 1998). The music therapist works with clients in the areas of relationships and emotional and mental health, working to develop resources and skills in these areas that will allow independence. Arthur (1999) notes the lack of attention given to the emotional problems that people with learning disabilities may have, particularly issues such as loss, grieving, mourning, bonding and attachment. Music therapy provides one way of working in partnership with people with learning disabilities to assist them towards developing greater emotional resources.

Music therapy work with adults with learning disabilities

This part of the chapter reviews music therapy work with adults with learning disabilities in the UK (see Patey 2000 and Jones 2005 for a history of the arts therapies and music therapy professions). Previous writing (Watson 2002) will be drawn upon to summarize work with adults with learning disabilities.

In early music therapy books, journals and newsletters in the UK, therapists wrote about their work with adults with learning disabilities. Most of the work initially took place in large hospitals. Writing of a directive style, using pre-composed songs and pieces, pioneer Juliette Alvin stressed the importance of the work, asserting that 'we know that music is an essentially flexible means of communication which can work at every mental, emotional and social level' (1975: 2). Wing stated that even with the most disabled of clients 'a thin link of communication has been forged' (1968: 8). Odell wrote of a developing model of British music therapy, stating that she worked 'always from the spontaneous music [the client] produced, taking up ideas in an improvisatory way, until he eventually made eye contact, and dialogue was possible' (1979: 13). Later, Odell-Miller reflected on her early working experience with these clients, stating that 'there wasn't anything in this country that was written down about adults with learning disabilities in a systematic way, about assessment or referrals', and explaining how she undertook a small research project in order to survey staff views about the benefits and effectiveness of music therapy (Odell-Miller and Darnley-Smith 2001: 9).

As work continued to develop in this area, Blackburn (1992), Clough (1992), Cowan (1989), Davies and Mitchell (1990), Gale (1989), Ritchie (1991), Sobey (1993) and Zallik (1987) documented work in the *British Journal of Music Therapy*. This important writing used case study format to describe the process of clinical work undertaken with adults with learning disabilities, documenting the developments in music therapy work during this time. Fischer (1991) and Clarkson (1991) also used case studies to document music therapy work. Sometimes this writing contributed to the development of theory within the profession, several of the writers introducing psychoanalytic concepts. Zallik's (1987) article argued for work with people with learning disabilities to be considered of equal worth as work with people with mental health problems, giving an interesting insight into the dynamics of the profession at the time. Gale's article captured the changes in the learning disability field at the time, considering the idea of normalization and the way in which music therapy could provide clients with a way of dealing with difficulties from the past and integrating more easily with others (1989: 23).

In 1988 Wigram explained how music therapy developed in this clinical area: 'the therapist is required to provide weekly sessions for groups and individuals who receive very little else', and how although 'referrals have often been made for all the wrong reasons', this enabled music therapists to develop specific skills and expertise in working with clients. Group work is also described in this paper. A useful description of the function of music therapy at that time is provided:

> Seeking to create or develop an alternative means of interaction is one of the primary functions in music therapy. The effect of providing this new means for a person to make contact and be understood has a profound value in satisfying emotional needs, and in building relationships with other staff and particularly with other mentally handicapped people.
>
> (Wigram 1988: 44)

Some authors described other approaches to music therapy with this client group (for example, the behavioural alleviation of physical symptoms). Hooper and Lindsay (1990) measured pulse rate and behaviour in order to ascertain the effect of music on anxiety, and Hooper et al. considered the effect of recorded music (1991). Both Wigram (1989) and Hooper (2001) have written about the use of low frequency sound in vibroacoustic therapy.

Although the 1990s saw an increase in the music therapy literature published, work with adults with learning disabilities was still infrequently documented. Ritchie described her long-term work with clients with severe disabilities and challenging behaviour, showing the way in which music therapy allowed two clients to develop relationships with other people and attain a higher quality of life (1993a). Both Bunt (1994) and Ansdell (1995) give a brief summary of adult learning disability work. The majority of literature documenting work with adults with learning disabilities is described in terms of a psychoanalytically informed approach. For example, in her chapter describing the process of work with a young woman with an eating disorder and Down's syndrome, Heal states:

> As a music therapist, I try to understand what meaning is held for the client in the improvisation, their use of the musical instruments, and the physical movements. This is all within the context of our developing relationship. The emotional impact of the relationship on me is used as a tool in making sense of the client's internal emotional life. I seek to understand, to reflect and interpret musically, or verbally, therapeutic issues that have particular relevance for the client. This can also be described as trying to explore with the client the links between their feelings, fantasies and behaviour. This provides the opportunity for real change to take place.
>
> (Heal 1994: 280)

Other writing considered assessment (Grant 1995), and in the same volume Heal-Hughes again used a psychoanalytic model to compare mother–infant and client–therapist interactions (1995). Chesner (1995) described the use of fairy stories in a dramatherapy and music therapy group for adults with learning disabilities.

More contemporary authors have been able to draw both on this existing body of music therapy literature and on new ideas and debate within the field of learning disabilities. Walsh writes about work with an adolescent (1997), Atkinson describes her work with a man with autism (2003), Usher writes about her work with people with profound learning disabilities and the idea of neuronal assembly formation (1998), and Hooper *et al.* (2004) write about the link between music therapy and sensory integration, and the importance of working with the multidisciplinary team. Richards and Hind bring attention to the concept of secondary handicap and the theories of Foulkes and Winnicott in their writing about group work (2002). Watson and Vickers (2002) write about their work with clients in music and art therapy groups focused on specific themes, which include a visit to Tate Britain gallery as part of the work. Watson gives a picture of the work of the music therapist with adults with learning disabilities (2002), and Darnley-Smith and Patey's (2003) book includes case study illustrations of the work of the music therapist with these clients. Wigram *et al.* summarize the principles of work in Europe, stating that 'the primary therapeutic goals . . . involve working with contact, communication and sensory stimulation. Music and musicality as a tool can evoke the expression of feelings and emotions in people with physical and developmental delay' (2002: 169). Townsend examines development of different music therapy theories, noting both the distinction between the importance placed on the relationship with the music therapist through music, and the relationship with the music itself, and the importance of understanding the impact of the client's learning disability. She considers that 'in working with clients with limited expressive and receptive language and whose capacity for cognitive thought and therefore, insight, may be impaired, the experiential aspect of the therapy is often the most significant' (2004: 38).

Research

Music therapy is still a relatively young profession and much of the debate in the area of research focuses on finding appropriate research methodologies, and on finding or developing tools to collect and analyse data and effectively evaluate the work. Although research and research literature are growing steadily, there are currently no standardized research or evaluation tools for music therapy work with people with learning disabilities (see Ansdell and Pavlicevic 2001; Wheeler in press; Wigram *et al.* 2002). Methods that have been used in music therapy research across various client groups have been both quantitative and qualitative, and have included random control trials, video and musicological analysis. Clinical and professional issues have been studied. In recent years, the advent of evidence-based practice has meant music therapists need to show the efficacy of their work. Edwards considers this, including the difficulty of using randomized control trials in music therapy researching (2002, 2005). Jones considers the issue of efficacy across the arts therapies (2005).

Little research has been with adults with learning disabilities. Such research as has been published includes a small outcome study of work with women with mild and moderate disabilities and the effect of music on anxiety (Hooper and Lindsay 1990). Hooper's subsequent (1993) project responded to a critical review of music therapy literature and described a project using music therapy and control sessions with a woman with learning disabilities. Oldfield and Adams (1990, 1995) compared the efficacy of music therapy and play activities in achieving specific behavioural objectives for adults with profound disabilities. In 1995 Toolan and Coleman studied the levels of engagement and avoidance within music therapy sessions with five moderately learning disabled clients.

Woodcock and Lawes, also writing in 1995, document a project that showed no reduction in self-injurious behaviour as a result of music therapy. Their considerations of issues raised by the design and undertaking of the research are useful (in particular they discuss the methodology and model of music therapy used). Wigram has written about several research projects: first, with adult clients where positive and negative behaviours were measured during sessions (1993a); second, the effects of low frequency sound on anxiety for clients with challenging behaviour (1993b). In this writing Wigram reflects on the ethical and methodological challenges of researching this work. Graham's research with preverbal adults uses transcription to analyse the musical therapeutic relationship, and concludes that vocal work 'can play an important part in establishing and developing a therapeutic relationship in which clients' communicative skills can grow' (2004: 27).

Consent to participation can pose a difficult issue for researchers in this clinical area. This issue has been considered in some detail in recent years (Kellett and Nind 2001; Kiernan 1999; McCarthy 1998; see Emerson *et al.* 2004 for a comprehensive presentation of international research). Kiernan asks if a 'new paradigm' model of participatory research, or cooperative enquiry, is appropriate when researching with people with learning disabilities in order to find out their views. He states that research carried out by non-disabled interviewers 'runs the serious risk of people with learning disabilities giving answers which they feel are required of them rather than their true views' (1999: 47). Kiernan considers that participatory research would still exclude a proportion of clients who have severe or profound disabilities. McCarthy considers how informed consent might be sought and outlines some of the difficulties of gaining evidence of informed consent such as a written or verbal record (1998). Dye *et al.* also consider this issue, suggesting that 'in some circumstances an individual could participate in research if they were assenting to the research procedure' (2004: 149). The Mental Capacity Act aims to give clear guidance for research with people who at that time cannot make their own decision about involvement (DOH 2005a; see also DOH 2001a, 2001b).

This chapter has given an overview of the history and diagnoses of learning disability, considering the key issues for adults with learning disabilities. Music therapy work with adults with learning disabilities has been introduced, and a review of the literature given. The chapters that follow provide a detailed picture of the work of the people with learning disabilities in music therapy, using clinical vignettes to illustrate points of theory and practice.

Music therapy with adults with learning disabilities

Sharing stories

Tessa Watson

> Fundamental to the practice of music therapy is the idea that the emotional world of patients is complex, full of good and bad experiences and is intact, regardless of the degree of intellectual difficulties or handicap.
>
> (Toolan and Coleman 1995: 17)

Music therapy clinical work

This chapter describes music therapy clinical work with adults with learning disabilities in detail, using composite clinical examples to illustrate key themes. Referral, assessment, treatment and the ending of therapy will be considered.

Referral

A referral to music therapy will usually come from someone who has noticed something about the person and their life that needs help; sometimes the person themselves will seek help. People are referred to music therapy with very different needs (see Box 2.1). Often common referral themes are to do with communication and interaction (see points 1 to 5 in box), or clients may come to music therapy because of experiences in their lives that are causing unhappiness or distress. Every client is different and brings us a new story to share. As Hollins describes: 'each person feels that they are a person first, whatever other people think. Of course each of us is aware of our difference from others' (1997: 3).

David, Tom and Nasser

Three imagined people with learning disabilities, their therapists and networks of carers and family are now introduced. We will follow their process in music therapy through the chapter. Interspersed with their stories are points of reflection on theory and practice relevant to the work.

Box 2.1 Reasons for referral to music therapy

1   Difficulties in making and maintaining relationships or meaningful interaction.
2   Difficulties in relationships with others, such as repeated aggression or lack of self-confidence.
3   Difficulties related to communication.
4   Difficulties related to sensory impairments.
5   When the client is experiencing a period of difficult emotions (for example, are worried, upset or angry) and it is hard for these feelings to be communicated through usual ways of communicating such as talking or signing.
6   When there is a specific issue for which the person needs help (such as bereavement, anger, a response to a life event).
7   Following the experience of multiple losses (for example, the death of a parent and a subsequent house move).
8   When a person has experienced abuse (for example, physical, sexual, emotional, neglect).
9   When there is behaviour that challenges staff and services.
10 Where there is an additional mental health problem.

David

David is a 24-year-old man referred to music therapy by Jamal, his day centre key worker. David has profound and multiple learning disabilities and physical disabilities, and is preverbal. He uses a wheelchair and needs help in all his everyday activities. Jamal made the referral because he felt David was frustrated in his efforts to communicate with others, and he wanted him to have an opportunity to communicate in a different way. Jamal has noticed that David is alert and aware of all that is going on, often using his voice to make contact with others in the day centre.

Tom

Tom is a 32-year-old man with autism and possible mental health problems who has recently begun a part-time college placement after having spent years at home during the day. Tom has a lot of energy and is finding it hard to know how to use this energy to make contact with others. He finds the busy college environment difficult. On occasions he is aggressive and distressed when with others, and he has assaulted another student who tried to help him calm down. Tom's college tutor spoke to Tom, his mother and care manager about these difficulties, and together they have made a referral to Carol, the music therapist.

Nasser

Nasser is a 52-year-old man with a moderate learning disability, who attends a day centre. The day centre is changing, with outreach projects that involve exploring the community. Nasser has found this difficult, and it has brought up issues for him about what his learning disability means for him, his family and those around him. His confidence has diminished and he is refusing opportunities to go out in the community. One of the senior staff at the day centre has discussed the referral to music therapy with Nasser, who is considering whether he wants to meet John, the music therapist.

Reflection on practice – consent

Consent is an issue to be considered at all stages of the therapy process. Whilst parents of children can give consent on their behalf, from age 18 an adult should be consulted about all procedures, and has a right to refuse. No one else can give consent on behalf of an adult (see DOH 2001a, 2001b). People coming to music therapy should therefore be as informed as is possible about what will happen, in order that they can make a decision about attending.

Clients may not be able to sign a form or verbalize that they consent to treatment, but they may show their willingness or wish not to attend in other non-verbal ways. Accessible information such as charts and symbols can aid understanding and allow the communication of decisions about consent to treatment and use of illustrative records such as videotaping.

David's referral

Sarah took David's referral to the team meeting where new referrals are discussed. Here she discovered that the speech and language therapist knew David well, and the community learning disability nurses are also involved due to David's ongoing physical health needs. Sarah talks more with these colleagues after the meeting, as well as with David's home carer. Discussing a referral in this type of confidential setting ensures that all disciplines are informed about the work of colleagues, and also allows a group of people working with the individual to think together about what treatment might best help.

Sarah next meets David and Jamal to discuss the referral. At this meeting she completes documentation that gives a background to the referral. She finds out about David's everyday and family life, his culture, health, contact with other health professionals and any previous therapy. She tells Jamal more about music therapy and finds out what his expectations are for David's music therapy. Sarah spends some time with David as he takes part in an activity session. She notices that he is very interested and aware of all that is going on, but has few ways of contributing actively to the session. Following this meeting Sarah comes back to the team base to write her notes and to read the multidisciplinary file that documents David's care. All this preparation gives Sarah a context for the work she might do with David, and ensures she is not working in isolation.

Reflection on practice – clinical note writing

It is usual practice for music therapists to write process notes after each session. These are a full description of the session, including the therapist's personal feelings and reflections, and are often kept in a music therapy filing system. In addition, music therapists usually contribute in some way to a central or multidisciplinary file held to document the person's care. The formality, amount and content of these entries varies depending upon the setting; national and local guidance is available for therapists working in statutory settings (DOH 2003b; 2005b Annex A). Music therapists who do not work in a formal team setting often make links with local learning disability services (such as a community team or social services department) in order to establish lines of communication regarding mutual clients. Multidisciplinary notes are considered confidential, meaning that only those people closely involved in the care of the person will read them. Writing and keeping clear notes ensures not only that there is an accurate record of the therapy, but also provides protection for the therapist should any issue require an audit of the work.

Tom's initial appointment

We now join Tom as he is about to come to the music therapy room for the first time, for an initial appointment. Carol has met Tom and was able to observe some of his anxieties at college. She has spoken to Tom's mother to gain more information and has sent her some information. His college tutor, Janet, has also met with Carol, the music therapist, to discuss the referral. Carol sent Tom a Makaton symbol letter to explain this meeting, which he has read with Janet.

An initial appointment gives the therapist and client a first chance to find out if music therapy could be helpful. Usually lasting between 20 and 30 minutes, it gives opportunities to meet the therapist, see the room and try the instruments, and have an experience of what might happen in music therapy. The therapist might say something about music therapy and why the person is there, if this seems appropriate. They might introduce some ideas about what could happen in music therapy, demonstrate some of the instruments and offer a chance to play.

The music therapy room where Carol works is in a community centre. In the room there is a selection of instruments carefully laid out: a low table with some small percussion instruments on it; some larger instruments such as a xylophone, cymbal, temple blocks and conga drum and a piano. Carol chooses instruments that have a good sound, a range of different sound qualities, are from different cultures and can be easily played by clients with different physical needs.

For this session Carol has selected some of the instruments but has put others away in the cupboard, as she does not want to overwhelm Tom with new objects. Writing about psychotherapy with people with learning disabilities, Bates says that 'I like to "feel my way" at the beginning to try and find the "key" to a successful engagement' (1992: 83). Likewise Carol has strategies in her mind, but does not know how Tom will react to the music therapy setting. Her chosen strategy will respond to Tom's way of being in the moment. Carol may introduce some music, or some of the instruments, providing structure, or she may respond fluidly to Tom's spontaneous use of the time. Darnley-Smith and Patey consider the continuum of musical structures that the music therapist might use, ranging from tightly structured music to free improvisation (2003: 80). Carol's choices will be determined by her experience and musical personality as well as by the needs and context of each client.

Tom comes into the room and is immediately interested in the instruments. He picks up a shaker without greeting Carol, and begins to use it in a characteristic autistic 'flapping' way. Carol accompanies Tom's music with some singing and drum playing of her own. Tom looks up in pleasure, and their duet develops from this point of contact. Tom becomes excited and moves around the room trying different instruments, enjoying Carol's changing improvised responses. Then he suddenly appears overwhelmed and rushes at Carol, raising his arm as though to hit her and pushing over instruments and chairs. He wants to leave and takes his coat and rushes to the door. Carol waits as Janet talks to Tom, helping him to feel safe and encouraging him to stay if he can. Tom is not sure, but then makes a decision to stay. He is now calmer and plays for the remaining 15 minutes of the session.

After this initial appointment, during which Tom has shown how he might use the therapy productively, and also how his feelings can quickly escalate out of control, Carol suggests that Tom and Janet take some time to decide if Tom would like to come back for a series of assessment sessions. Carol writes detailed notes; not only an account of what happened in the sessions but also how she felt in response to Tom's use of the appointment. She formulates aims for the work, thinking about congruence between the reasons for referral, Tom's use of the appointment, and the opportunities that music therapy can offer. After a week, Carol rings Janet to ask how Tom is getting on with making a decision. Janet is enthusiastic and says that Tom would like to come, so a series of six weekly assessment sessions are arranged.

Reflection on practice – assessment

An assessment gives both client and therapist more of a chance to see how the music therapy session could be of use. The length of an assessment can vary, but a guideline for assessing people with learning disabilities is between four and eight sessions. This reflects the time that it can take some people to adjust to a new setting and new worker.

When planning an assessment, music therapists consider practical issues such as the most useful way to arrange the instruments and how to introduce them to the client; whether a structured or freer approach would be most appropriate, and the way in which the client will be most usefully supported to attend sessions. Throughout the assessment, the therapist will maintain a 'questioning and explorative stance' (Hodges 2003: 43), thinking about whether the client can develop a useful working relationship with the therapist (a therapeutic alliance), whether music therapy is the right approach at the right time, and whether individual or group work might be most useful. Some settings offer multidisciplinary assessments including a music therapy component (Oldfield undated; Wigram 1988). This allows for a holistic approach and gives the person opportunities to indicate preferences for a particular way of working.

Reflection on practice – boundaries

Boundaries of relationship and environment help therapy to be used to its fullest extent, and may vary depending upon individual needs. Sessions are usually offered once weekly (sometimes twice a week), for an agreed length of time, in the same room. Often, the therapist will arrange the room in the same way each week so the environment can become familiar. Therapy work requires privacy and it is important that sessions are not interrupted by others.

The length of a session may vary: for individual sessions from 20 minutes to 45 minutes, and for a group between 45 to 60 minutes, for example. Regular sessions of the same length and at the same time are important, as this reliability can become internalized and anticipated, even where people are not able to note days or times. Using the whole session, rather than finishing early or starting late if the person does not use all the time actively, allows the therapist to share all of the client's experience. Other boundaries or rules relating to behaviour towards the instruments, therapist and group members may be negotiated in order to ensure the most positive and safe use of the environment.

Therapists may adapt these basic boundaries to help the person use the session or maintain the therapeutic alliance. If the therapy environment presents challenges to a client they might begin therapy by attending for a shorter length of time, extended gradually. Likewise, if a client uses behaviour that challenges, a session may need to end early. It is particularly important in this area of work to reflect on relaxed or adapted boundaries to ensure people with learning disabilities are being valued sufficiently to allow them a regular, uninterrupted time. Sometimes discussions around time boundaries and issues of attendance may need to take place with carers who are supporting the person to attend, as well as with the person themselves.

Nasser – starting a group

In a city day centre, John is discussing the possibility of a new group with the manager, Bernie. John has noticed that recent moves towards community access have unsettled some service users who find this challenging. Bernie and John discuss the fact that as the users gain more independence and use the community more, they also confront the idea of difference directly, and can experience comments or attitudes which make them painfully aware of their disability. John wants to offer a music therapy group to support these experiences. John writes aims for the group and discusses it at the staff meeting, collecting referrals. He then meets each person with their key worker or carer at an initial appointment. Nasser is one of the first referrals, and he decides he would like to attend. Other referrals come from the community team, for people who do not access any services and are living in isolation in the community.

This group will run for an hour each week for 2 years, and Nasser will attend regularly. His anxieties and fears about being in the community will be vividly conveyed through his use of the group.

Reflection on theory

> Human beings have an inner world as well as an outer one, an unconscious as well as a conscious, and therefore those with a handicap need just as much attention to these aspects of life as others.
>
> (Sinason 1992: 74)

As described in Chapter 1, one way of working in music therapy is with a psychoanalytically informed framework. Early life experiences impact on how we live our adult lives and are given particular importance in this way of working. By the time we are adults, patterns of communicating and ways of being with others are well established and we may need to help to change these. A psychoanalytic framework helps therapists to think about clients' ways of being in the world and patterns of relationships with others, and some central concepts will be considered here. More has been written in recent years about the use of psychotherapy with people with learning disabilities and this literature is useful to the music therapist (Beail 1989; Hernandez-Halton *et al.* 2000; Hollins and Sinason 2000; Simpson and Miller 2004).

The conscious and unconscious

The term conscious describes the part of us that is aware of what we are feeling, thinking and of how we are making decisions. The term unconscious describes the emotional parts of ourselves that are outside our awareness, but nevertheless have an influence on how we behave. People with learning disabilities have a conscious and unconscious life but are unlikely to articulate this concept. However, they may come to music therapy because someone close to them has noticed that they have a pattern of behaving that prevents them living a fulfilling life.

Transference

Unconscious patterns may be brought into therapy through transference. This term refers to the way in which a past way of relating is brought into the present moment; 'a living memory of the patient's early relationships with important figures, experienced in the here-and-now relationship with the therapist' (Hernandez-Halton *et al.* 2000: 120). For example, a client may bring an expectation that the therapist will always choose instruments, initiate the music and make all the choices; perhaps a transference of an authority or parental figure. These past ways of relating can be given special attention in a therapeutic environment.

The feelings that arise in the therapist as a result of transference are termed countertransference. Priestley describes this as follows: 'The countertransference may come to the therapist's awareness through an uneasy question of "why am I doing/saying this?" and a vague feeling of acting out of character, not once, but over and over again with this one particular patient' (Priestley 1994: 85).

In learning disability work it is not always possible to check these feelings with the client. The therapist therefore needs to reflect carefully on her feelings, and discuss them in supervision. Casement tells us that 'therapists need to acquire their own capacity for spontaneous reflection within the session, alongside the internalized supervisor. They can thus learn to watch themselves as well as the patient' (1985: 33). In music therapy work, transference and countertransference will arise as part of the therapeutic relationship and therapists may choose, according to their style of working or the needs of the person, how much attention to pay to these. Therapists working with an awareness of these concepts might use music or words to address issues that arise.

Defences

Attachment theory (Bowlby 1979) makes us aware that people with learning disabilities may experience difficult patterns of attachment in their lives, and may use psychological defences as a way of managing these. Defence mechanisms help us to suppress or deny that which is unacceptable to our conscious thought, thus avoiding emotional conflict. Defences are therefore healthy, but their rigid or overuse can lead to unhelpful patterns of behaviour. It is not the therapist's job to remove these defences, particularly in work with adults with learning disabilities where a sense of self can be fragile, but an important function of our music is to contain unbearable anxieties and unacceptable feelings. We can think with clients (and in supervision) about what defences might mean to a person and how things might change in order that they can start to use their resources differently and live more fully.

Some defences employed by people with learning disabilities arise from a negative sense of self. This may have its origins from birth, when perhaps the family is shocked and grieving at the birth of a baby with a disability and find it hard to value their child. A sense of a person being less valued can be unconsciously communicated by family, peers, workers and the community. People with disabilities may be aware that society wishes to prevent disability. Music therapy gives an opportunity for disability and the impact it has on lives and relationships to be explored: 'people may need long-term and patient condolence and support with deep emotional upset at their internalized perception of themselves as "impaired" and "a problem"' (Race 2002: 60).

Secondary handicap

Linking with the idea of defence, Stokes and Sinason (1992) have written about the concept of secondary handicap (see also Hartland-Rowe 2001). They use the term to mean the consequence of a learning disability and describe three types: secondary handicap, opportunist handicap and handicap as a defence against trauma. This concept considers how people may use their learning disability, consciously or unconsciously, in order to hide their real feelings, defend against painful feelings of difference, and manage the fact of their learning disability. Hernandez-Halton *et al.* state:

> Reality is difficult. There is no way around this fact. One of the difficulties is to acknowledge and live with one's limitations. We all have them, but having learning disability makes these limitations more

concrete: a person with learning disability is more of a receptacle for other people's projected feelings of limitation, rejection and other unwanted negative emotions. Dealing with the reality of disability and life can be too much for some patients and then a secondary handicap may emerge.

(Hernandez-Halton *et al.* 2000: 121)

Mother–infant theories

Theories of mother–infant interaction provide useful frameworks for the music therapist. In 2000 Stewart found that 71 per cent of music therapists who responded to his survey gave this as a theoretical model that they used. Mother–infant theories can be particularly relevant to work with clients who are preverbal and need help to build intentional, reciprocal and creative relationships. This work is documented in detail in Chapter 8, where the idea of Stern's concept of affect attunement will be considered (1985). Theories of holding, environment and play (Winnicott 1958, 1960, 1971), and containment and reverie (Bion 1962a, 1962b) may also be helpful to the therapist working with adults with learning disabilities. Speaking of psychotherapy, Winnicott states:

Psychotherapy takes place in the overlap of two areas of playing, that of the patient and that of the therapist. Psychotherapy has to do with two people playing together. The corollary of this is that where playing is not possible then the work done by the therapist is directed towards bringing the patient from a state of not being able to play into a state of being able to play.

(Winnicott 1971: 44)

This may also be the role of the music therapist who works to develop playful, creative relatedness through musical interaction.

David

We rejoin David after three months of individual therapy. David and Sarah are nearing the end of a session, and their music is in full flow. David is using his voice to create long lines of sound, and Sarah is accompanying and developing his music using her clarinet. Their music is spontaneous and communicative and Sarah feels that the individual sessions have met a number of aims. They have allowed David to engage closely in an individual relationship, building his confidence in his own contributions in a relationship, and have given him an opportunity to share his feelings. She is now considering offering David a place in a small group in order to develop his ability to relate to his peers.

Reflection on theory – music

> An instrument will not retaliate and cannot be hurt. It can contain all
> manner of projected feelings, even those very uncomfortable and
> destructive ones that are difficult to verbalize.
>
> (Bunt 1997: 255)

Therapist and client are active partners in music making in a therapy
session. As the therapist responds to the material (musical or other) that the
client brings, she works to find a musical way to be with the client,
supporting and facilitating musical expression. Sobey and Woodcock note
that 'following the client does lead to a quite specialized form of musical
behaviour in which the therapist's personal musical/emotional impulses are
held in check' (1999: 140). The music made with adults with learning
disabilities will be varied, as with other clients, but there may be particular
characteristics. The therapist may find that she is working with very little
material (for example, when working with clients with profound and multiple learning disabilities). This demands that the therapist is able to wait
and listen, avoiding playing to fill the silence rather than in response to the
client. Other clients, whilst bringing music, may find it hard to initiate or
lead music, leading to fragility in the contact between the therapist and
client, where the therapist may feel as though they have complete responsibility for sustaining the music. At times the therapist may need to call
upon all her musical resources to keep the music alive and fresh. Supervision provides a space to think about these issues, and to gather thoughts
and ideas to take back into the clinical work.

Although the UK model of music therapy uses mainly improvised music,
therapists usually retain flexibility in their use of music to meet the needs of
the client including, for example, the use of pre-composed music, familiar
songs, song work and taped music. Part of the therapist's role is to think
creatively to provide the optimum musical environment for client/s, an
environment that will inevitably develop and change during the process of
therapy.

Nasser's group

We meet Nasser again when his group has been running for a year. The
membership has changed gradually, with three people leaving and two
people joining during the year (this type of group is sometimes called a slow
open group). The group has some basic musical structures at the beginning
and end of each session to help the group to focus and greet each other, and
the central part of the session consists of loose often alternating structures
of musical improvisation and talk. The group decide how to use the time,
who might play and what is played, and their starting point is usually news

or thoughts that group members bring to share. From this, imaginative music and talk emerges.

Nasser uses the instruments with enthusiasm, both sharing positive feelings with his friends in the group, and expressing difficult feelings such as anxiety and fear. His confidence in the group has grown and he has forged positive, supportive relationships. He has been able to use the group to think about how it feels for him to leave the day centre, and has been able to engage a little more with the community experiences that are offered. A group such as this has a broad remit of developing and maintaining positive mental health:

> Mental health includes a positive sense of well-being; individual resources including self esteem, optimism, a sense of mastery and coherence; the ability to initiate, develop and sustain mutually satisfying personal relationships and the ability to cope with adversities . . . Mental health also affects our ability to cope with and manage change, transition and life events.
>
> (Foundation for People with Learning Disabilities 2002: 11)

Reflection on practice – words

Work with adults with learning disabilities demands that careful consideration is given to the way in which language is used, whether clients are verbal or preverbal. The amount and content of speech used can be moderated depending upon the needs of particular clients. It is important not to overwhelm people with inaccessible language, and therefore music therapists may think a lot more than they say. Talking may arise naturally from the music, instigated by clients or therapist. If words are accessible and non-threatening, talking about feelings may help to clarify or explore a feeling or situation. Pelham and Stacy speak of words as a way of 'translating the content and process of the creative medium into the verbal medium and thus acting as a bridge between the two media, facilitating continuity and coherence' (1999: 17). In a group setting, the opportunity for sharing thoughts and having group discussion can be a valuable way of learning how to work as a group and support each other.

Words are used in a functional way (to mark the passing of the session time, to explain a break, to offer an instrument), as well as to think about the music and the issues that have arisen. Makaton symbols and charts are a valuable adjunct to words and can help information and ideas to be understood where words are not sufficient. In addition, the *Books without Words* series (Hollins 1993–2005) explores concepts and feelings about issues such as bereavement, moving house, going to hospital and abuse.

Responding to the needs of the client may mean that words are used infrequently during music therapy sessions. Where this is the case, it is useful for therapists to find ways to articulate their thoughts and feelings outside sessions (e.g. in process notes and in supervision).

Reflection on theory – group work

The music of the therapist or of the group may, like the well-attuned mother, offer a means through a medium other than words by which the patient can feel recognized. That recognition also allows things to move forward.

(Davies and Richards 2002: 18)

Group participation is sophisticated and complex and it is not surprising that many adults with learning disabilities find it hard to take a full part in group settings. Foulkes and Anthony remind us of the importance of groups when they write: 'being a respected and effective member of the group, being accepted, being able to share, to participate, belong to the basic constructive experience in human life' (1984: 27). Group therapy gives people a way to think about themselves and their relationships in a setting that can represent their wider life. A group allows members to experience different roles – leader, supporter, listener, soloist – and thus to explore different ways of being with others. A music therapy group has particular value for people who find it difficult to work with words, as it allows them to be equal members of the group through their musical contribution, and to explore roles and issues without needing verbal fluency.

In work with these clients the music therapist is likely to take an active role at first, perhaps demonstrating instruments, providing ideas and musical structures, and musical and verbal guidance when required. The therapist is usually able to adopt a less directive approach as the group find their own way of working together.

The following writers have contributed to thinking about the role of the music therapist in a group. Stewart writes of the importance of the therapist providing 'availability and resilience in a reliable presence week by week', an 'enlivening, alerting presence' and 'a source of spontaneity and surprise' (1996: 25). Glyn describes that the therapist might 'support the music by reinforcing and developing what the patients are playing. They try to draw out the more coherent and organized elements whilst noticing and responding to the quieter and more disparate parts' (2002: 51). Odell-Miller writes of enabling 'meaning to develop through this process [of playing music], and to think constantly about what might be happening in the playing, as well as when there is no music'. She reminds us that 'interactions are played out within improvisations; the therapist must recognize this and not avoid issues she perceives or hears' (2002: 64–5). Some music therapists also find it useful to draw on theories of group work from psychotherapy and group analysis. For example, Bion (1961) writes about the unconscious processes that occur in every group (the basic assumptions of dependence, pairing and fight or flight) and Vinogradov and Yalom give a useful summary of research into the therapeutic factors of group psychotherapy (1989).

Tom – ending individual therapy

When we meet with Tom again, he has attended six assessment sessions and a further ten treatment sessions. Following this phase of therapy Tom, his college tutor Janet, and Carol the music therapist have met to think about what might happen next. It is clear from Tom's engagement in music therapy that music is a powerful medium for him to manage his energy and aggression. After each session Tom has been calm and settled but it has been hard for him to take this experience back to the college environment. Tom has decided that he does not want to continue to come for more music therapy as he wants to attend college full time. Together, Carol, Janet and Tom think about ways in which the insights gained from music therapy might be used to help at college. They consider strategies such as a person-alized box that contains instruments, music tapes or videos that Tom can use when he needs to manage the stress of college. Janet keeps in touch with Carol after therapy has ended to let her know how things are going for Tom. This joint evaluation with the client and a carer is a useful way to monitor the progress that has taken place in music therapy.

Reflection on practice – supervision

> The struggle to stay with something painful, however small, is hard enough for the worker, and often impossible for the child [adult].
>
> (Sinason, 1992: 146)

When therapists work with severely disabled clients in long-term therapy, supervision has particular importance. The client's primary disability will not change, and their life situation may not change significantly. Sometimes a therapist may experience a feeling of exhaustion or boredom when working with such clients, and supervision is important in helping the worker maintain thoughtfulness and freshness. Therapists may experience feeling cut off from the work, or difficulty in staying focused in the therapy; something that Sinason describes when she finds herself thinking about her shopping list in work with Steven, a man with severe learning disabilities: 'Steven was being as good as dead precisely so I could think about shop-ping lists, or indeed anything except him' (1992: 127). Levinge considers the powerful nature of musical material and suggests that 'the raw emotion, which arises out of the therapeutic relationship and cannot be put into words, may mean that this particular clinical material can be most difficult or painful to bear' (2002: 88). Supervision with a suitably qualified and experienced therapist is important in helping music therapists to sustain this work.

Consideration of support networks in the work setting is also a useful part of the supervisory process. Not only individual workers, but also learning disability services can become identified with their clients' disabilities and find it hard to develop and remain lively and creative in their thinking. Staff may identify with clients in feeling unvalued, as though they have decisions imposed upon them rather than having choice. A peer supervision or discussion group in a work setting can allow staff to share positive and negative feelings about the work, value their work, support each other and also learn about each other's roles. Brown and Smith talk about the importance of this in relation to the concept of normalization:

> Services which use normalisation need to be robust enough to take on board the negative feelings which workers have about the work they do. The alternative is to bring in fresh young workers, fire them up with idealism and then watch them leave when they find they can no longer contain the feelings aroused in daily contact with people who are sometimes difficult, boring, dangerous and sometimes lovely, lonely, lively or depressed – in short, human. Because ambivalence is at the root of all human relationships and because service workers relate to people in less than ideal situations and with a half-hearted mandate from society at large, they must be allowed space and freedom from censure in acknowledging how they feel.
>
> (Brown and Smith 1992: 89)

Reflection on practice – endings

In some work, endings come about naturally. The work to be done in therapy may be clearly finished – perhaps a child leaves school or moves into a different class, a patient is transferred to a different ward or leaves a hospital. In work with adults with learning disabilities we may need to be more active in making an ending where there are few natural transitions. Managing a planned ending in the supportive environment of therapy can be a useful rehearsal for managing other endings in life. Mattison and Pistrang state that this is 'crucial if clients are to develop new relationships in the future' (2004: 165). Discussing the therapy at the ending in an evaluative way with the client (if possible) and carers allows insights to be shared. Carers can find new ways of working with the person and learn about their skills or abilities. Thus, the client's total environment is enriched, as well as personal development having taken place.

The chapters that follow illustrate music therapy clinical work with people with learning disabilities through the presentation and discussion of detailed case studies.

Chapter 3

Music therapy and autistic spectrum disorder

Rhian Saville

This chapter gives an overview of autistic spectrum disorder (ASD), outlining its common features and causes. The relevance of music therapy with this client group is explored and a case study illustrates a typical piece of work.

What is autistic spectrum disorder?

Autism is a complex, pervasive developmental disorder that is present for life. It affects the way a person communicates and relates to others, and can be wide-ranging in terms of how it impacts on their life. First described in 1943 by the Austrian psychiatrist Leo Kanner, the typical features that characterize autism for modern day diagnoses such as *ICD-10* (World Health Organization 1992) and *DSM-IV* (American Psychiatric Association 1994) are now known as the triad of impairments (Wing 1996). These difficulties typically affect a person's social interaction, communication and imagination. Other features that are often present include a desire for sameness, repetitive behaviours and resistance to changes in routines.

Whilst these defining criteria provide clear guidelines for diagnosis, each child or adult who presents with an autistic disorder has their own unique characteristics. It is therefore recognized that there is a 'spectrum' of autistic disorders that encompasses many levels of intelligence and ability. For instance, individuals may vary in their social skills, with Wing describing four typical groupings of social impairments: aloof, passive, active but odd and over-formal, stilted (Wing 1996). As difficulties in communication are common, the person's use of speech and understanding of verbal and non-verbal language can also vary widely.

An autistic person's ability to play is significantly impaired, as there is a lack of imagination within their activities. Toys or instruments are often used as objects that may be twiddled or flapped to create an interesting physical sensation. Repetitive actions or routines can develop into stereotyped behaviours such as spinning, rocking, clapping and staring at bright objects. These can take the form of movements and patterns which serve as a reassuring or calming sensory experience for the individual, or give a sense of order in an otherwise confusing world.

The spectrum of autism is therefore wide-ranging, and there are sometimes additional disorders that are present or develop during the person's life. These can include learning disability, epilepsy, sensory sensitivity and psychiatric illness. Along the continuum lies Asperger's syndrome. Defined in 1944 by Hans Asperger, this is characterized by many of the same features as autism, such as difficulties with communication and social interaction. However, the individual with Asperger's has not usually experienced a delay in language or cognitive development and has an average or higher level of intelligence. Unlike autism, there is often an interest in other people, but the person with Asperger's displays peculiarities in their use and understanding of verbal and non-verbal language. Similarly to autism, there is a need for predictability and routine, but the marked stereotypical behaviours are not so prevalent. A person who has Asperger's also lacks the ability for imaginative play, but can develop almost obsessive interests in certain topics. This often involves memorizing facts about subjects that are generally predictable and non-emotive in nature, such as trains, animals or birthdays (Frith 1991).

What are the causes of ASD?

There has been much debate over the cause of autism and Asperger's, with various psychological and biological theories being postulated. The psychogenic notions of Bettelheim (1967) and Kanner (1973) imply that a child develops autism as a result of an uncommunicative, emotionless 'refrigerator parent', whilst the Tinbergens (1983) believed in the case of maternal anxiety leading to infantile autism. In contrast, cognitive theories suggest that brain deficiencies are the primary cause of autism (Rutter 1983; Coleman and Gillberg 1985; Steffenberg 1991) and much thought has been given to genetic factors (Folstein and Rutter 1977; August et al. 1981; Rutter et al. 1990; Szatmari and Jones 1991).

Cognitive theories explaining the causes of autism were developed further through the notion of a 'theory of mind' (Baron-Cohen et al. 1985; Baron-Cohen 1995). This suggests that people who have autism lack the ability to 'mind-read', or understand the thoughts of others. This theory has significant importance in understanding the minds of those with autism, as it highlights how the person's cognitive impairments impact on their interpersonal interactions. Thus, in not knowing that other people have mental states that may be different from their own, the person with autism has difficulties in relating to and communicating with others. As Happe states:

> We make sense of behaviour in terms of mental states. Without such a "theory of mind", the social world must be a terrifying, unpredictable

place. No wonder the autistic child often fights against it, or withdraws from it physically or mentally.

(Happe 1999: 49)

Other cognitive concepts have been put forward towards an understanding of autism. The first is that of central coherence, which is defined as global processing (for instance, remembering the essence of a story but not the finer details within it). It is suggested that individuals with autism display a weak central coherence (Frith 2003), so that details are focused on without reference to wider meaning. Executive function is the second theory relating to cognitive impairment. This is the prefrontal capacity to plan and control attention to an activity, thus enabling one to attend to more than one thing at a time (Frith and Hill 2004). Poor executive functioning is typical for a person with autism, so that they might perseverate on a task without being able to move on or initiate a change in the activity. This is very commonly seen in the musical or social play of an autistic person.

A combined theory of the origin of autistic spectrum disorder has also been debated over the years. For instance, Tustin (1986, 1992) acknowledged that there may be organic causes to ASD but she also suggested that psychogenic factors such as the infant's relationship and attachment to its mother are key factors in autistic states. Similarly, Alvarez (2002) explores the notion of an 'interactional' model of multiple causation in which both organic and psychoanalytic theories may influence each other. Also more recently, psychoanalysts such as Hobson are arguing a socio-environmental model in which the development of human minds is a result of interactions between the infant and its caregiver (Hobson 2002).

Why music therapy?

Music therapy is widely used with people who have ASD. Much evidence exists in the literature on the effectiveness of using music to facilitate communication and interaction with this client group, although the majority of published articles and books are based on work with children rather than adults. For the purposes of this chapter, reference will be made to both areas, as the principles outlined for children can be applied in the main for adults.

Key innovative works by Alvin and Warwick (1992) and Nordoff and Robbins (1971) described how the power of music could be used in the treatment of autistic children. Alvin states: 'I used the compelling power of sound to penetrate and to provoke in the child conscious or unconscious responses, hoping that music could not only reach him, but help him to reach out, in a two-way process of communication' (1992: xi).

Brown elaborated on these initial ideas by detailing four main points that explain why music therapy is 'such a vital therapeutic tool in working with people with autism' (1994: 18). First, she aligns musical structures with elements of organization and creativity that are required for a person's functioning in the world. The elements of music can also be used to help develop social relationships, along with musical sounds such as pitch and rhythm being interpreted by the therapist into purposeful emotional communication. Finally, Brown asserts that because music is directly related to emotions. It can 'provide access to a wide diversity of emotional qualities, with a directness of connection that can bypass cognitive thought and language' (1994: 18).

Bryan also refers to the elements of music created within a group for autistic adolescents, in which 'the group experienced producing something together in a shared mode of expression about a shared experience of autism' (1989: 20). She believes that through this group encounter the students were able to begin the process of understanding their own sense of self; a concept explored further by Tyler (1998), who describes the musical and therapeutic processes of two autistic children through the notion of Laing and Winnicott's true and false self. Di Franco (2002) also writes about the different aspects of an autistic person that can be expressed through music, in this case vocally.

A comprehensive overview of music therapy for children with autism is given by Robarts (in Trevarthen *et al.* 1998). After a detailed literature review she discusses the current phenomenological and psychodynamic debate in music therapy practice, and how this impacts on the field of autism. An in-depth case study of a young boy with autism demonstrates how musical improvisation based on models of mother–infant interaction helped to develop the child's socio-emotional experience. Woodward (2004) specifically aims to develop the parent–child relationship within a family-based approach to working with autistic children and in doing so offers emotional support to the parents involved.

Recently, music therapy has been combined with other therapeutic approaches for specific reasons. Social stories are musically adapted in Brownell's research (2002) to help autistic children understand social situations or events, whilst Berger (2002) describes a collaborative approach between music therapy and sensory integration theory with autism. This text explores the physiological functions of an autistic person and how a music therapist might address sensory needs through the elements of music.

In children's services, music therapy is currently being used as a diagnostic tool in the field of autism (Wigram and De Backer 2002; Oldfield 2005). Wigram and De Backer state: 'Music therapy can play a very significant role in the assessment process with children who have communication disorders, because of the non-verbal nature of the medium when working with pre-verbal communication systems' (2002: 70).

Here Wigram outlines a framework for assessment using a combination of structured and unstructured improvisations to elicit responses from the client. As well as analysing the musical material and interactions within the sessions, he observes the child's physical and tactile behaviour, pathological elements in the music, and social interaction and communication. Autonomy and variability scales from Bruscia's improvisation assessment profiles (Bruscia 1987, cited in Wigram and De Backer 2002) form the basis of the assessment, which enables a diagnosis of autistic spectrum disorder to be made if appropriate.

Oldfield's tool, as yet unpublished, suggests some useful and interesting methods. Similar to Wigram's approach, a mixture of free improvisation and directive musical activities form the basis of the assessment sessions. Scorings are made on the child's musical and social engagement, stereotyped activity and imaginative ability, in order to inform a diagnosis of ASD.

Whilst the tools developed by Wigram and Oldfield are primarily designed for the diagnosis of children, there is potential to adapt them for use with adults. Both authors conduct their diagnostic assessments in conjunction with a multidisciplinary team involving psychiatrists, psychologists, nurses, social workers, etc. and this may be similar for music therapists in adult services.

Although the published literature available on music therapy with adults who have ASD is fairly sparse, the range of approaches described is quite diverse and reflects something of the nature of the work with this client group. First, Clarkson's (1991) account of a two-year case with a non-verbal autistic young man outlines her improvisatory Nordoff Robbins approach alongside both behavioural and psychodynamic orientations. She incorporates instrumental playing and dancing within clearly structured activities to meet the aims of developing communication and self-expression. Activity-based methods are also central to Wager's (2000) work with an adult autistic male. Here pre-composed musical songs form the basis of instrumental and vocal tasks that serve to meet the aims of building skills in the areas of interaction, self-expression and choice making.

In Toigo (1992) the personal insights of Dr Temple Grandin (an autist) are combined with current music therapy practice. In her writings, Grandin refers to music and how it is effective with people who have autism, particularly when it is combined with movement-based activities. Three basic treatment recommendations are suggested based on Grandin's experiences. First, there must be a sense of structure, both within the music and in the session as a whole; Second, improvised music should reflect the client's physical movements, musical pitches or emotional qualities in their sounds, to convey 'acceptance and understanding' of the person with autism (1992: 19). Grandin is also an advocate of sensory integration theory (Ayres 1979, cited in Toigo 1992) and she believes that music is effective in providing appropriate auditory, proprioceptive, tactile and vestibular stimulation for the autistic person.

The link between music therapy and sensory integration is explored further by Hooper *et al.* (2004). Here a multidisciplinary approach to addressing the sensory needs of an adult with ASD and severe learning disabilities is made through an activity-based music programme. Hooper also advocates for the combined media of music and movement with this client group to address physical as well as psychological needs.

In contrast, Graham's approach is wholly centred on the emotional world of her clients (2004). Her research focuses on music therapy with a preverbal autistic adult where vocalization is used to establish an interactive relationship. Here early infant communication models are used so that every musical, physical and emotional response is interpreted and reflected within the improvised music. By 'tuning in' to the expressive quality of the client's sounds, a trusting relationship was formed and communicative and social skills were seen to develop.

To summarize, the use of music therapy within this field is wide-ranging. At the core lies the need for an approach that addresses the emotional, social and communicative needs of the person with autistic spectrum disorder. In addition to this, music can be used effectively within the scope of sensory integration and social stories. Finally, yet to be developed with adults but already in use with children is the implementation of music therapy as a diagnostic tool within multidisciplinary services.

What are the main reasons for referral?

Many of the referrals for adults who have ASD that are made to the service in which I work are typical for those who have a learning disability: namely, to help in the areas of communication, self-expression and social interaction. In addition to these, however, are often more specific reasons for music therapy assessment and intervention being appropriate to the needs of an autistic person. Examples may be as follows:

- behaviour difficulties such as aggression, isolation, withdrawal
- extreme anxiety or ritualistic behaviours
- support around coping with change, such as transition
- specific emotional support, for example, around bereavement
- sensory issues, such as an interest in auditory/tactile/visual stimuli or difficulties around repetitive self-stimulatory behaviours
- need for an outlet for physical as well as emotional release
- a love of music, where the person can usually be motivated or calmed by music.

What are the common strategies?

Since the pathological needs of adults who have ASD are often very similar, it can be useful to think about particular strategies when working in a music therapy situation. However, it is stressed that these strategies are by no means exhaustive and other factors may influence the musical and therapeutic relationship between client and therapist. The next part of the chapter outlines some of the generic ways in which to approach this work.

First, I would describe my clinical approach as being informed by a combination of musical, developmental and psychodynamic models. It is necessary to consider all three models when working with adults on the autistic spectrum as each has relevance to the therapy. So, in thinking about appropriate ways of engaging a client, all these theories will be referred to.

Structure

The first issue to consider is structure. As with all effective therapeutic approaches, boundaries of time, place and environment are essential to maintain consistency and stability in the formation of a therapeutic relationship. For autistic adults, these are vital. If necessary, symbols, photos or pictorial timetables can also be used to reinforce the predictability of the music therapy sessions, thus providing a tangible means of security for the client. Within the sessions, a clear sense of structure can be achieved through the use of beginning and ending songs or activities, as well as similar patterns of musical activity (either improvised or directive) being present each week.

Therapeutic relationship

The therapist also needs to be comprehensible and predictable for the autistic client in order for a trusting relationship to develop. Many adults on the lower end of the autistic spectrum communicate with Makaton signs and symbols. If this is the case, then it is important that the therapist is consistent with this way of communicating. Music therapists will also find it useful to familiarize themselves with some of the many texts written by people who have autism or Asperger's (Williams 1996; Lawson 2001) in order to increase their understanding of the condition and for practical ideas on how to communicate effectively with this client group.

Because the main features of ASD involve a lack of emotional relatedness and impairments in social understanding, the therapist should consider psychoanalytic concepts such as transference and countertransference when establishing a therapeutic relationship. These concepts are the windows to the client's world of emotion and relationships and will inform the work along its journey.

Musical interaction

The musical relationship creates a shared experience of interacting in the here and now. Whether it is through pre-composed or improvised music, the therapist's goals should include the development of preverbal interaction skills, such as *timing, imitation, tuning in, eye contact* and *intentional initiation.* By encouraging these elements of early communication, reciprocal dialogues can be created within the music and therefore give the client an experience of shared social interaction. Stern's theory of affect attunement (1985) is relevant here, where the therapist mirrors and develops any form of communication from the client. The rhythms of rocking, flicking and tapping that are often so isolating for an autistic person can be incorporated into the musical dialogue, along with the emotional and musical qualities of vocalization. Timing is crucial, as the therapist must allow the client to process the musical and social information that is being presented, thus giving them space to respond.

To promote attention and interaction, it is sometimes useful to share an instrument, either sitting or standing opposite the client. Commentary songs improvised about the person can also be effective. These give opportunities for direct eye contact as well as imitation or turn-taking dialogues with the instrument or voice. Percussion instruments such as tambourines and drums are useful for this as the sounds can be easily controlled. Cymbals, wind chimes and ocean drums are often really motivating for an autistic person as they are aesthetically interesting – their shiny surfaces are fascinating and ideal in which to absorb one's attention. Whilst these may be a useful starting point in a music therapy session, the therapist must be aware of the possibility that the instrument might become an autistic object. If they have the sense of the client becoming absorbed in the instrument, their intervention can be adjusted accordingly to regain their attention.

Once a musical interaction is established, a common experience for the music therapist is that of perseveration. Thus, the client may now have become stuck in their playing or activity so that the compulsivity that drives the behaviours causes a withdrawal into their own sound world. They may be absorbed in the sensory stimulus of the sounds or movements that are being produced. The aim for the therapist is now to find ways in which to challenge this avoidance through musical change or variation so that the process is a creative rather than an isolating experience.

Whilst it is not helpful to be prescriptive about which instruments or techniques are most useful, it is important to bear in mind that if the therapeutic aims when working with a person who has ASD are centred around social interaction, communication and imaginative play, then the therapist must be mindful of the tendencies of the client to withdraw into their own typical mode of being. Thus, extra attention should be paid to promoting these aims to their fullest potential.

Emotional containment

Central to any music therapist's work is that of emotional containment. This notion, described by Bion (1962a), suggests that the mother (or therapist) hears the child's expression of his difficult feelings, experiences them for herself, processes them and then responds. The feelings are therefore worked with in a safe, unfrightening way. When a person on the autistic spectrum is not able to make sense of their emotions, the skilled therapist can use an appropriate musical framework to contain and work with them.

Sensory integration

Many children and adults who are on the autistic spectrum have some sensory sensitivity or difficulty in processing sensory information (Attwood 1998). This can be in the areas of any of the sensory systems: tactile, vestibular, proprioception, visual, auditory, gustatory and olfactory. Music therapists such as Berger (2002) and Hooper *et al.* (2004) advocate the use of music in facilitating sensory integration. Their work is activity based and collaborative with the multidisciplinary team (in particular occupational therapists and physiotherapists, who may have specific training and experience in sensory integration theory). Specific instruments and songs are used to work with the client's touch, movement and motor planning, whilst the elements of sound, rhythm and texture are considered in relation to the person's sensory needs.

If the person displays particular sensory difficulties, this behavioural approach can complement other more psychodynamic ways of working. By addressing the physiological as well as emotional world, music therapy can help minimize behaviours that hinder a person's ability to focus and communicate with others.

Case study – James

James is 32 years old and was diagnosed with ASD at the age of 25. It was felt he had developmental delay from the age of 3. The main features of his autism are as follows:

- difficulties in social interaction and communication but also enjoyment of contact with others
- makes strong attachments to key people and experiences separation anxiety
- has a tendency to be 'egocentric'; needs to impose his own will
- repetitive behaviours and obsessions, in particular touching and washing
- compulsive behaviours, usually related to high levels of arousal, which can develop into highly aggressive, destructive or self-injurious actions
- sensory difficulties, notably hypersensitivity to sound and touch
- neurological damage (possibly from medication or self-injury).

James was referred to music therapy for creative therapeutic input and assessment of his sensory issues. He was living alone in a specially con- verted flat in a unit for adults with learning disabilities. There had been a recent increase in his complex ritualistic behaviours, and he displayed enormous levels of distress and self-injury such as screaming and head banging. Physical closeness to other people often triggered compulsive, dangerous actions such as pulling hair and grabbing out at eyes or arms, so he was constantly maintained at a safe distance from staff and peers.

Close liaison with the multidisciplinary team was crucial. As issues of safety were paramount, care plans for the management of James's moods and behaviours were shared. The range of the team's therapeutic approaches was important in helping to understand and support his emotional world. The network provided a much needed forum of support during challenging times for all staff involved. The initial aims of therapy were:

- to build a positive relationship between James and the music therapist
- to offer an expressive outlet for James
- to encourage James's creativity and play through music
- to explore creative ways of helping James cope with his obsessions.

Extract from assessment period

The sessions are in James's flat. For my own safety, we are placed either side of a wall separating myself and James. A small hatch similar to the opening between a kitchen and dining room is positioned at waist height in the wall; small objects can be passed through it. A reinforced window above the hatch sits at head height. I play percussion instruments softly through the hatch. James sits to one side of the opening so that he is hidden from my sight. Small vocal sounds emerge through the hatch. James is listening and showing some musical response to the instruments. A sound is suddenly heard from another part of the building. James immediately jumps up, shouts and bangs his fist on the wall between us. I sing 'banging doors', meeting the sudden change of emotion. James joins in, singing loudly, and moves forward, peering at me around the hatch.

Reflection

James is motivated by the music and is showing an interest in me. His physical positioning is interesting as he is choosing when to be seen and is directing our interactions. He shows an ability to imitate pitches accurately in the music, and shares a variety of moods and emotions. A lot of infor- mation about James's sensory difficulties is being noted. He has auditory sensitivity and attempts to calm his proprioceptive system by banging walls, hitting himself or jumping.

Extract from development period

James is in the middle of his lounge, dancing to music on a CD. I am dancing on the other side of the wall, and we occasionally catch sight of each other through the small window. James sings loudly and expressively until the end of the song when we both sit in a poignant silence. A noise is suddenly heard from outside. As before, James jumps up, screams and bangs the window. His mood has changed dramatically and he rips his shirt as he strips off his clothing. I suggest putting the CD back on. The screaming gradually subsides and his attention is drawn back to the music. He sits down and continues singing as I pack away the instruments.

Reflection

A wide range of emotions were expressed during this period. James's musical play was developing and he engaged through playing instruments, singing and dancing. The 'pop star' play was becoming a feature which expressed many feelings. James's confidence and esteem were high during these interactions as he explored various roles and imagined himself visiting nightclubs and having girlfriends. The music that was shared helped to focus James through more difficult moments and contain his outbursts in a safe way. He was now more able to work through his compulsive responses to external noises. Suggestions were made that the team could help James access his music during the week to allow him an experience of being in control of his auditory environment.

Extract from continuation period

There has been a break due to my maternity leave. James and I are facing each other, on either side of a half open stable door. During my absence staff have worked hard to increase contact with James and he accepts closer physical presence. Our session is therefore conducted over the door and I am struck at how physically close we are to each other. I realize for the first time that he is taller than me, and wonder what he is feeling. He chooses the large drum and I lift it over the door. We begin playing a steady, rhythmic pulse together as I sound the tambourine. A call and response dialogue develops, becoming louder and more energetic. James is focused on our music and the improvisation lasts for 20 minutes. I change to flute. James begins dancing and exuberantly singing "Who's playing? It's noisy!". I warn him that the session will end in five minutes. As we gradually quieten he stops, sustains eye contact and offers his hand out to me. As I place my palm on top of his, he smiles.

Reflection

Closer physical contact had an immediate effect, with James able to express himself in more ways with larger instruments. His attention was more focused on our playing, and at once the length of the improvisations doubled. The contact between us felt close both musically and interpersonally, and James communicated his feelings about this by initiating positive physical contact with me for the first time.

In Ogden's description of the autistic-contiguous mode of being he states that 'it is experiences of sensation, particularly at the skin surface, that are the principal media for the creation of psychological meaning and the rudiments of the experience of self' (Ogden 2004: 52). Here a significant connection was made as James initiated touch between us, as if symbolizing the musical connection or 'touch' that had occurred through our rhythmic and vocal contact.

Major changes were happening in James's life, ultimately preparing a move to a converted house. After years of isolation these were enormous achievements for James and he continued to use the safe music therapy setting to make up stories about what might happen. His confidence and esteem continued to rise and he shared these feelings in our improvisations.

Extract from new community period

James has moved to his new home and I am waiting for him to arrive for music therapy at the new day centre venue. He comes bounding through the front door exclaiming, "I've got a new house!" In the music therapy room we begin a drum and guitar duet, which is rhythmically strong and full of turn-taking. It feels as though we are having an animated conversation. James catches sight of the keyboard and begins to sound clusters of notes. He turns the volume to maximum and holds the keys and pedals down. He is completely absorbed and unaware of my attempts to play with him. His music is so loud that I cannot hear my sounds at all.

Reflection

James's house move was mirrored by the transition of music therapy to the day centre. This gave opportunities to access larger instruments such as the keyboard, piano and drums. We were interacting on a more equal level, sharing the space with no physical barriers between us. It felt significant that a drum could be placed between us, and James imitated my rhythms and hand movements with accurate awareness. The music was often intense and James played for 30 minutes as though he needed every moment available. He often chose the keyboard and surrounded himself with a deafening wall of sound. My experience was of James being remote and difficult to engage with. It seemed as though he was creating his own defence now that the physical barriers had been removed. This way of playing also appeared to provide a satisfying sensory experience for James.

There were now moments when I had to consider my own safety, which had been previously protected by the physical environment. Although James had never been aggressive in music therapy, it felt as though there was potential for his mood to escalate out of control and I was in a constant state of alertness to this. Sometimes a member of staff sat in the room to help manage this risk and this affected the dynamics between us. Nevertheless, it was important to continue to provide a therapeutic space and relationship for James, to witness his music and support his means of coping with the major changes occurring in his life.

Present

It is now a year since James moved to his new home. He has coped well with the transition and the accompanying staff changes. Music therapy has been one of the few constants through this period and has provided a sense of stability for James. He has expressed a wide range of moods and emotions through his music, and now through words. He names feelings such as 'sad' and 'happy' and talks about his anxiety regarding changes to his routines, such as when our sessions have to be cancelled. Whilst his behaviour can still be volatile, James is managing safely in his house and he feels a real sense of achievement. His sense of self is continuing to develop and during the most connected moments in our music he has exclaimed 'I'm a man!'

Conclusions

Music therapy has proved to be an important therapeutic space in which James has explored and shared his feelings in a creative way. The musical relationship has supported the extremes of mood, emotion and behaviour evident in his difficulties in social interaction, communication and self-expression. The compulsiveness and sensory sensitivities that led to his isolation from others were acknowledged and worked with, and imaginative play was encouraged and supported through musical improvisation.

Most important, however, was the emotional support that developed. At a time when James was physically and socially isolated from others it was vital that he had an opportunity to engage in a positive and safe therapeutic relationship. Music could traverse the unusual boundary of a wall into his flat and 'touch' him emotionally, beginning a shared dialogue that helped James express something of his experience. Through vocalization, instrumental improvisation and movement the musical relationship was created, and imaginative stories and roles were explored to prepare for the move to a new placement. Psychoanalytic concepts of transference and counter-transference played an important role in understanding the processes that were evolving. It has been useful to consider how the trust and stability within our relationship has impacted James's developing sense of self.

The progress in James's music therapy can be paralleled with early stages of infant developmental models, from the womb-like experience of his initial environment to the first encounters through vocal response. Musical dialogues developed through imitation and play, and James began to verbalize his feelings. As our relationship grew, so did James's attachment to me. As his sense of self continues to develop, he is showing more confidence in choosing instruments and directing our playing as well as sharing thoughts and feelings.

Music therapy continues to provide containment for James's emotions each week. Our work is moving into its next phase as he establishes his life in the community. There are many unknowns on this journey, but our musical relationship remains a constant that accompanies James along the way.

Chapter 4

Challenging behaviour

Working with the blindingly obvious

Cathy Warner

Challenging behaviours are best thought of as being a way in which people respond and try to gain control over difficult situations.

(DOH 2001c: 103)

Introduction

This chapter explores what we understand by challenging behaviour, factors which influence this phenomenon and approaches that music therapists use with people who are affected by challenging behaviour. What does challenging behaviour mean? The term has been used by health and social care professionals primarily in tandem with the label of learning disabilities, although as implied by the quotation above, challenging behaviour could be produced by any of us. It includes a wide range of actions: self-injury, violence to others, frequently running away, deliberate incontinence, and undressing in public. There are many more examples. These actions cannot be easily ignored. As others in the vicinity are generally provoked to respond, it may be helpful to think about challenging behaviour within the context of *relationship*.

Challenging behaviour as a social construct

Labels for people with learning disabilities have tended to be evaluative and imply deficiency. Sinason (1992: 39–54) explores how and why euphemisms for the differences implied by handicap have mutated into terms of abuse throughout history. But why is it that these terms tend to be more evaluative than those of other types of difference, for example, labels of ethnicity (Abberley 1992)? Although 'challenging behaviour' is an attempt to label the person's actions rather than the person, it still carries the implication of judgement. The contemporary expression 'behaviour which challenges the service' attempts to shift the label on to an organization or sector of society. However, to become labelled 'with challenging behaviour', one must have developed a reputation for behaving outside socially defined norms. Inescapably, 'challenging behaviour' is a social construct applied most frequently to vulnerable people.

Ways of thinking about challenging behaviour

In the research literature about challenging behaviour, the main emphasis is on self-injury, possibly because it is the most distressing aspect. Anyone who has seen someone hit their ears until they bleed is not likely to forget this experience. There has been some interest in theories about endorphin production as a result of some self-stimulation or self-injury, which can be pleasure inducing. However, the significance of environmental factors is slowly gaining prominence (Murphy 1994; Hare and Leadbeater 1998). Notably, children with 'normal' development can show behaviour such as head banging at certain developmental stages (Emerson 1995: 60).

In 1993 *The Mansell Report* was published (DOH 1993), a substantial review of services for people with learning disabilities and challenging behaviour in Britain, informing the later government white paper *Valuing People* (DOH 2001c). It recognized a wide range of factors influencing challenging behaviour, including physiological aspects such as epilepsy, sensory impairment and physical illness. The report also included a number of circumstantial factors: a history of neglect and/or abuse, a reputation for past challenges, a restrictive home environment, carers not understanding the meaning of the behaviour, overemphasis on risk reduction, low expectations from carers, and the absence of verbal language. All these factors would be of interest to the music therapist seeking to understand the meaning of actions that a client shows in a session.

The Mansell Report stressed that good practice occurred when workers tried to use 'information about *individual experience* as a primary organising force in their work' (DOH 1993: 3, emphasis added), and encouraged client-centred approaches such as music therapy.

Service provision

The Mansell Report found that 'even moderate levels of challenging behaviour are not being appropriately managed in mainstream learning disability services, and specialist services (including some of dubious quality) face apparently unlimited demand' (DOH 1993: 3). The report was sympathetic to the difficulties carers faced, acknowledging that more progressive services could place higher demands on an already very difficult job. Care staff may also be under immense stress, due to role ambiguity and role conflict, exclusion from decision making and having unreachable demands placed on them (Holt 1995). They are more likely to move into flight–fight reactions to residents' communications because of these high stress levels (Lally 1993). However, many carers find the work rewarding, despite feeling undervalued (Bell and Espie 2002).

There is evidence that a move to the community has improved some lives. The prevalence of self-injury has reduced (Murphy *et al.* 1993), as has the use of psychotropic medication and restraining devices. Although occasionally communicative and challenging behaviours increase, some research attributes this to an increase of opportunity for self-expression, activity levels and communications (MacLeod *et al.* 2002).

Behaviour, communication and meaning

There are a number of approaches to challenging behaviour that have influenced music therapy practice. The strategy of ignoring the behaviour and instead reinforcing positive interactions within the music is quite widespread practice, clearly influenced by behavioural theory. *Valuing People* mentions 'modern behavioural approaches' (2001c: 103) as an effective option other than medication for helping people manage their challenging behaviour. However, researchers who have used cognitive-behavioural approaches with people with learning disabilities recommend they are used with people who have good verbal skills (Kushlik *et al.* 1997) excluding others lacking these skills.

A music therapist with a humanistic underpinning is likely to consider challenging behaviour as communication. Responding to such communications in music by improvising in an empathic manner, possibly using similar sounds and body postures, allows the client to experience an acknowledgement of their feelings and communications. One specific example of this outside music therapy practice is the use of the intensive interaction approach (Hewlitt and Nind 1998). Here carers respond to such communicative behaviour by using brief but intense non-verbal contact in an attempt to build up mutual communication.

In addition music therapy practices may also consider the symbolic meaning of the behaviour. This may be particularly powerful when the behaviour is quite disturbing. For example, one man repeatedly broke his legs by throwing himself from his wheelchair (Lovett 1996). Eventually the doctor in charge, in what seemed to be an act of despair, decided to amputate his legs. This addressed none of the fundamental issues the man was communicating but stopped the presenting problem in a profoundly unethical way. Lovett interpreted the repeated injuries as symbolic of a desperate need for closeness, as this man had been institutionalized from infancy and only experienced intimacy from his carers following his injuries. Had a music therapist been available, they could have used a musical relationship to explore a more positive attachment experience. To use symbolic interpretation, music therapists need to be clear about the theoretical background they draw upon, in this instance, a psychoanalytic model. More recently culture-centred approaches (Stige 2002) have gained prominence in practice and involve the therapist understanding challenging behaviour in relation to the cultural and social pressures the client is under.

Whether one takes a specific model or an integrated approach, I believe it is helpful to identify whether there are any symbols, communications or behaviours which seem invisible or have become taboo. Sometimes behaviour is so shocking or disturbing that paradoxically we defend ourselves against the communication or feeling by ignoring it. Surprisingly often, these behaviours are forcefully and frequently re-enacted. A decision to ignore behaviour so that it is not reinforced may prevent us from hearing and therefore understanding what the client needs to communicate. A critical awareness of our own responses may help prevent us ignoring what may be 'blindingly obvious'.

However one decides to understand or manage challenging behaviour, the focus of music therapy is invariably on the individual needs of the client rather than the behaviour. Often a client is referred because of challenging behaviour, but the focus of the therapy becomes an exploration of the underlying reasons for the behaviour, rather than an attempt at a cure.

Examples from the music therapy literature

Although little has been published about music therapy in this specific field, most examples come from therapists who are influenced by psychoanalytic theory, in particular, the concepts of secondary handicap (Sinason 1992), as described in Chapter 2, and attachment theory (Bowlby 1979, 1988). These may help in understanding why someone who has lived in a hospital since infancy may have such difficulty relating to others. Ritchie published powerful case studies of her work with people with profound learning disabilities (Ritchie 1991, 1993a). She described how she used music therapy over several years to support people who were in a high degree of confusion and distress. Ritchie felt that her clients were unable to believe that anyone wanted to communicate with them. This work took place just before the move towards community living. In the 1990s music therapists were often involved in supporting clients in the preparation for a move towards community living. Ritchie's case studies gave hope that music therapy could help people find confidence in the value of relating to others.

Research in music therapy with this client group is rare. One exception is the study conducted by Woodcock and Lawes (1995), using a randomized controlled trial design to investigate whether music therapy with adults with severe learning disabilities would diminish self-injury. Although this was not confirmed, the authors comment upon several benefits of the musical therapeutic relationship. Many music therapists feel that rather than specifically aiming to reduce self-injury, a music therapist may best serve their clients by trying to understand, acknowledge and influence the emotional factors which underpin such behaviour.

Anthi Agrotou (1998 and 1999) follows the course of a music therapy group for four institutionalized women with profound learning disabilities and their carers, working towards a move to community care. This four-year case study was set in a long-stay institution in Cyprus, as opposed to Ritchie's work in England, but many of the issues are similar. Agrotou draws detailed attention to what meaning the actions of the women clients might communicate, concluding: 'Whatever the person's degree of disability and deprivation, every minute signal carries a meaning; and that person's desire to be reached and share his/her world transcends their cognitive, physical and environmental difficulties' (Agrotou 1998: 251). This model of attempting to understand and interpret the meaning of sometimes very tiny actions is one that may be adopted by music therapists who use varied theoretical approaches: the therapist must be critically aware of the way their own theoretical model shapes their interpretations. In this group, carers took a fundamentally active role and became 'facilitators on the route to becoming auxiliary therapists' (Agrotou 1998: 68). The carers showed signs of having internalized aspects of Agrotou's conceptual frameworks through what she calls 'unconscious observational learning'. This contrasts with music therapy models where carers adopt more passive roles.

Clinical example

The following case study follows three men with severely challenging behaviour. Peter, Jack and Bill were members of a music therapy group run for five men at their community home. The case example explores the changes which occurred for individuals within the group process rather than focusing on the dynamics of the group.

Background

All five men had lived all their adult life in large hospitals. Furthermore, three of them had been institutionalized from infancy or early childhood, and it was likely that this history would have affected their opportunities to make good attachments to others.

Pete had lived at home until, as an adult, his illness and behaviour became too difficult to manage. He was strong, and as a result of his tendency to throw large objects, there were no moveable objects in the home, the kitchen was locked and the television was bolted down.

Jack, apparently severely autistic, had been institutionalized from the age of four. Avoiding most human contact, he had little sense of the distinction between private and public. The challenge for others was to spend more than the most fleeting time with him.

Bill was terminally ill with cancer and in fact died later in the year. Due to his particular needs, special attention was paid to his choices about participation in the music therapy group.

All five men had lived together on a hospital ward for 14 years and had been the last residents to transfer into the community. None of their original care workers chose to move with them. Their unhappy situation was not helped by the hostility of some neighbours in the local community. Because of the perceived risk entailed by all five travelling together in a minibus, therapy at home was the only option available. Music therapy began six months after the move. The music therapy group, although closed and confidential, formed the focus of a detailed piece of participatory action research involving the residents, care workers, the music therapist and the home managers as co-researchers. Although I was not the music therapist, my role was as facilitator to the inquiry process, and I brought to it my perspective as a music therapist. The inquiry took place over the period of a year and was divided into six research cycles.

The music therapy process enabled the men to move from suspicion and avoidance of relationships towards the creation of a sense of community and relatedness. In a parallel process to the therapy, the music therapist and I worked with carers to challenge perceptions of the residents, and identify and confront what we were tending to ignore. Descriptions of meetings with carers are in italics.

Cycle 1: encounter

Sessions 1 to 4

Although chairs were arranged in a circle, residents did not always sit down and play but wandered in and out of the room. The music therapist gently sang the name of each resident after they had been in the room for a little time, using an improvised modal song. This acted as a commentary about who was in or out of the room, and allowed the therapist to invite and explore tentative connections with each person. However, the frequent changes caused by people wandering in and out gave a sense of a lack of containment. One inquiry participant wrote: 'There is no *idea* of community.' Pete constantly hovered at the door, unable or unwilling to cross the threshold. Jack sporadically wandered in and out, occasionally handing instruments to the therapist but not making sounds himself.

In the second session Bill was angry that a chair had been brought in from the dining room. However, the therapist had decided not to remove it. Bill then began to try different ways of getting rid of the chair. He tried pushing the chair, screaming, pushing the therapist and finally hitting other residents. This vivid experience of such a rapid transformation of communication powerfully illustrated, as pointed out by some participants, how unbearable the experience of not being heard might be.

In the first staff meeting some participants were angry that Bill had been caused distress by a refusal to move the chair. The therapist felt Bill was well enough to deal with therapeutic challenge. Others saw this as his particular brand of challenging behaviour, others as an attempt to spoil the session for others. This led staff and therapists to think about what it might be like to have therapy in one's own home and how it might be quite disturbing to have furniture moved around. Additionally, the sequence of strategies that Bill tried in response to being ignored forced us to think about Bill's history of disempowerment. The group decided to move the therapy away from the lounge where Bill rested, allowing him more freedom of choice to attend or not.

This example illustrates how the different perspectives on the meaning of Bill's actions led to disagreement and strong feelings but also a consideration of empowerment issues. Where there is challenging behaviour, a number of underlying issues may be usefully addressed within a well-facilitated team, using the mechanisms of reflective group discussion or team supervision. As the nursing employment structure within a community home is hierarchical, an independent facilitator might help address the power issues most helpfully.

Cycle 2: conflict

Sessions 5 to 7

Although Bill did not come into the new room, Pete began to attend. However, an underlying conflict became apparent between him and another resident. If one came into the room, the other left. The other group member tended to play music in short aggressive bursts. Pete did not seem to be able to work out how to make sounds on instruments, but he often pushed them. Pete tended to stand by the therapist as he sang, and his active participation as a listener became more apparent.

Cycle 3: exploration

Sessions 8 to 13

As Pete began to spend more time in the sessions, he started rolling drums across the floor to the music therapist and receiving them back. He stood by other group members when they were creating music, appearing to listen. However, he also started to throw instruments, seemingly in response to actions that aroused difficult feelings. For example, when Jack tried to take Nick's trombone away from him, Pete threw a metallophone across the room. The day care worker attributed this to 'attention seeking', and the therapist wondered about envious feelings and rivalry between the other group member and Pete.

In the staff meeting carers found it difficult to think about why Pete was throwing instruments, and remarked on the music therapist's tolerance of this. Rivalry between the two men highlighted a strength of feeling that had not been recognized before. One carer said: 'I thought that the men had no relationship with each other. Now I question that.' The focus of the inquiry began to shift from attendance patterns to an interest in the quality of communication and relationship between the residents. It was notable that this developed at the same time that relationships within the staff team became more trusting.

Cycle 4: envy and death

Sessions 14 to 23

Mutual music making between Pete, the therapist and another group member (Steve) became a regular feature of the group, although in Pete's case his participation was mostly in the form of supportive listening. However, he did begin to play the wind chimes and often used his voice during the music. Pete seemed envious of the quality of relationship between the therapist and Steve and began to throw large instruments more frequently to express this. Nick set down firm boundaries about what was acceptable in the group, at times asking Pete to leave for a minute. Pete quietly returned to the room soon after leaving, with his head hanging, apparently contrite.

Sessions 17 to 19 were dominated by Bill's distress and deteriorating condition, and it was then that Nick and Bill had the most musical connection, with Bill standing on the threshold of the room, but leaving if Nick moved towards him. Jack's attendance noticeably decreased, as if saying something for the group about how unbearable the feelings were in the house at the time. In the week of session 23, Bill was too sick to get up. All the other men were standing at the front door waiting for the music therapist to arrive. Such anticipation was unusual. That evening Bill died. However, none of the residents were involved in Bill's funeral which took place the following week.

The staff team were preoccupied with Bill's death and the events leading up to this, and they played very little part in the inquiry meeting. The music therapist and day care worker became quite concerned that staff members were preoccupied by their own grief, and were not always able to acknowledge the distress of the other residents, so apparent within the therapy.

Cycle 5: commitment

Sessions 24 to 34

Jack, who had only attended for brief periods, decided in session 30 to sit down and stay for the entire session. From this point onwards his commitment to the therapeutic process changed. He began to hum during improvisations, and started to offer instruments to other people in the group. He also developed some assertiveness by refusing instruments and moving chairs back if Pete moved them. The therapist wrote: 'This is a new way of Jack commenting on the effect Pete has on him. Usually he just leaves.' Others began to confront Pete, restraining him if they thought he was going to throw. Pete began to notice that his throwing damaged instruments, and although his throwing did not stop, it became infrequent. However, when he did throw, it was with great strength, and the therapist needed to set boundaries more firmly. As Pete began to listen more to others, so he had higher expectations of being heard. If the therapist did not respond immediately to Pete's singing, Pete would become angry. Pete's vocal sounds evolved from being a monotone sigh to a creative explosion of glissandi, crescendi and short punctuated notes, and he experienced other residents responding to these sounds in their own music. By this time improvisations often involved four or five people, an unexpected development from the fragmented music of the earlier cycles.

In the staff meeting, discussion centred on how the residents had been affected by bereavement, and how they needed to have been involved in a mourning ritual in some way. Some people were very surprised at the changes that Pete and Jack had made within the therapy group: and how complex group interactions were happening spontaneously. Although Pete's behaviour was becoming increasingly more challenging this cycle, all staff members appreciated that he was exploring different ways of being with other group members, and that this aroused strong feelings at times. Those in the meeting began to question why our expectations of the residents were often so limited. Jack's changes in commitment and assertiveness had been preceded by many tiny changes in earlier cycles which had gone largely unnoticed. Participants reflected that poor attendance did not prevent therapeutic change.

Cycle 6: intruder

Sessions 35 to 38

Five weeks after Bill had died, a new resident, Aidan, was moved temporarily into the home. Although Jack's involvement with the group continued to develop, Pete seemed very uncomfortable with Aidan, and generally stayed away. When Pete did come in, his throwing was much more frequent and violent than before and it seemed that he may have been protesting about the way that Bill had been replaced. Steve and Aiden started to lock Pete out of the room. Power issues were being explored with a new intensity.

The team discussed how the culture of locking doors, practised by all staff to keep Pete out of the kitchen, had been adopted by residents as a form of 'challenging behaviour' and how this might be changed. The powerful effects of bereavement on the residents were finally acknowledged and questions were asked as to how this might have been overlooked. Team members had to address the fact that it was often easier to ignore many of the very obvious communications of the residents, rather than hear them. These concerns motivated some policy change at Trust level, and had the effect of making some cultural changes within the staff group. At the end of the inquiry the music therapy group continued with a renewed confidence that this was a place in which residents could be heard, but also had begun to hear each other.

Summary

When the men were first referred to music therapy, it was evident that they had few opportunities to play, particularly with free-standing objects. Staff members believed that they had little relationship with each other, and found it difficult to stay with any activity for more than a few minutes. Cooperation and sharing seemed impossible to achieve when there was so little that seemed to capture the men's focus. The disruption and loss caused by the move and the men's past histories created enormous dis-advantages in their capacity to make relationships, and express feelings in a way that could be accepted by others. The music therapy group offered an environment where the men could explore their angry and jealous feelings about each other through musical expression, and later to articulate feelings of sadness about Bill's death. Although they started with great ambi-valence, Pete, Jack and Bill all found ways of exploring their relationships, first through a musical relationship with the therapist, and then through musical relationship with each other. The way the group was facilitated resulted in considerable freedom in participation, such as the choice of whether to stay or leave. Possibly as a result of this, each man began to choose greater involvement. This took time, an unsteady progress, but over the course of a year each group member had been able to make positive changes in their peer relationships. Apart from Bill, each resident had many experiences of the group creation of music, and increasingly began to feel that they could influence the shape of the improvisations.

This group illustrated how challenging behaviour can escalate quickly, as with Bill, and may be exacerbated by illness. Pete showed us that when therapeutic change is at its height, challenging behaviour can increase. Jack's transformation highlights how working with very small changes over time may lead to a dramatic reduction in challenging behaviour. The surrounding culture of a home may have an impact on the way power relationships are played out, as in the case of locking doors. Finally, the importance of firm boundaries helped Pete realize the impact his behaviour had on others, bringing about his will to change.

Conclusion

Challenging behaviour is a social construct which describes a phenomenon of great complexity and range affecting both clients and those in relationship to them. The challenge in practice is to try to understand the underlying causes. Music therapists may focus on a number of aspects: behaviour as communication, as a cultural phenomenon, the underlying symbolic meaning, detailed observation of minute change, involvement of carers in the music therapy process, reinforcement of positive musical behaviours or an integrated combination of these approaches. This chapter concludes with some suggestions for good practice in music therapy work with people with challenging behaviour:

1   Create clear boundaries.
2   Work with the individual rather than the behaviour.
3   Be aware of the capacity of music to highlight power imbalances.
4   Embrace a broad acceptance of what music can be.
5   Develop a critical awareness of cultural taboos surrounding the behaviour.
6   Be critically aware of one's own blind spots.
7   Use opportunities for collaboration with carers to try to gain a hold on the complexities.
8   Gain a detailed understanding of the individual's past (if possible).
9   Develop a good understanding of attachment and loss issues.

Chapter 5

'What bit of my head is talking now?'

Music therapy with people with learning disabilities and mental illness

Eleanor Richards

Historial considerations

In recent years there have been some profound changes in thinking and policy about the needs of people with learning disabilities. Some of the broader trends are obvious to the public gaze: the tradition of housing learning disabled people from an early age in large institutions, where they have had little contact with the wider community, has been replaced by a move towards community care and social integration. Implicit in that has been a recognition of the entitlement of learning disabled people to those ordinary aspects of living that the rest of us take for granted as necessary to our well-being: the possibility of active, flexible relationships, the exercise of creativity, the possibility of employment, and so on. Much of the most recent thinking in the UK is summarized in the White Paper *Valuing People* (DOH 2001c; see Chapter 1 of this book).

There have always been learning disabled people in all cultures, and society's responses to them have varied widely, from the impulse to end their lives in infancy, to allowing them to grow up into the 'idiots' who might become the objects of family and community teasing or shame, to placing them in institutions out of general sight. What these have in common, perhaps, is a focus upon the learning disabled person's oddness or inadequacy, seeing it as something to be managed, but not open to any kind of more complex curiosity.

In the past two centuries some broader thinking has developed about the possibility of mental illness in people with learning disabilities. As early as 1838 Esquirol, the French alienist (the nineteenth-century term for psychiatrist) remarked that 'idiocy is not a *disease*, but a *state* in which the intellectual faculties are never manifested or developed' (cited in Berrios 1994: 8, emphasis added). He saw idiocy as a disorder of the mind, and therefore something that alienists should take interest in, but not as a form of insanity. Perhaps this marks the start of the debate that continues today about the difficulties in distinguishing between phenomena that are innately indicative of learning disability and those that point to an overlay of mental illness. In 1835 the British alienist J.C. Prichard remarked:

> [Idiotism is] a state in which the mental faculties have been wanting from birth, or have not been manifested from the period at which they are usually developed. Idiotism is an original defect and is by this circumstance, as well as by its phenomena, distinguished from that fatuity that results from disease or protracted age.
>
> (cited in Berrios 1994: 12)

Later in the nineteenth century a line of thought emerged which emphasized a continuum between normality and disability, leading to the assertion that people with learning disabilities were not by definition mentally ill, but better thought about in developmental terms. While that rescued people from crude assumptions about 'madness', it also brought the risk that distressed behaviours might be ascribed to the fundamental disability itself, and so not open to the relief that psychiatric intervention might bring. Szymanski (1994) points out that clinicians generally have no particular hesitation in diagnosing mental illness in people suffering other forms of physical or sensory disability, whereas they continue to be much more cautious about people with learning disabilities. All this is more than an academic debate. The proper recognition and treatment of mental illness in people with learning disabilities is something to which they are entitled; it also has implications for service planning and social provision.

Perhaps the central difficulty in any discussion of this area is that both disability and mental illness may first be recognized through observation of behaviour. It might appear simple to say that in learning disability the general features of a person's functioning and processing may appear inconsistent with and less competent than the norm for someone of their age and background, whereas in mental illness it is the *quality* of those processes that suffers. But it remains that in many mental illnesses it is the level, rather than the quality of functioning, which appears impaired, perhaps adding to difficulty as to what phenomena may be attributable to disability and what to illness. It is confusions like these which have contributed to the tendency for many years to regard 'negative' changes in the behaviour of people with learning disabilities as merely further aspects of disability rather than as signs of deteriorating mental health.

It is only relatively recently that a specialism in the psychiatry of learning disabilities has become established, and although from the 1920s onwards there has been increasing recognition of the psychiatric needs of people with learning disabilities, that specialism remains small, and even in some western countries still has little representation (Hollins 2000). Difficulty in diagnosis is a central issue. Since traditional psychiatric diagnosis is often dependent upon patients' verbal accounts of their experiences, people with learning disabilities are at an obvious disadvantage. Doctors may be hesitant to make potentially far-reaching diagnoses based on limited direct communication with the patient (Szymanski 1994 makes a link with uncertainty about psychiatric diagnosis in young children). It is now recognized that more weight must be placed upon the observations and instincts of carers, and that clinicians working with people with learning disabilities need to use specialized assessment criteria (Royal College of Psychiatrists 2001). Cooper (2003) identifies the prevailing risk factors for mental illness in the general population and makes telling comparisons with the circumstances of people with learning disabilities. She suggests that biological, psychological, social and developmental factors are all potentially contributory to mental distress, and that consideration of them all should be central to the planning of treatment.

Specialist psychiatric services for people with learning disabilities have developed extensively in the past 30 years. Community learning disabilities teams now ordinarily include, or have ready access to, a consultant psychiatrist and learning disabled people experiencing acute mental health problems have greater access to beds in specialist units. These remain in short supply, however, and learning disabled people are still at risk of emergency admission in the first instance to general psychiatric wards, where they may not have immediate access to specialist psychiatric or nursing support. People with learning disabilities may experience particular difficulties in social functioning, which may in turn contribute to a deterioration in mental well-being. In recognition of that, many community teams now include social workers alongside a range of health professionals.

Biological factors putting a learning disabled person at risk of mental illness may include the psychiatric consequences of underlying genetic or neurological aspects of learning disability, epilepsy, physical or sensory impairments, and the side effects of medication. Developmental issues may include difficulty in communication, difficulty in understanding social norms, and patterns of behaviour normally associated with a pre-adult developmental stage.

These in turn play into a complex network of psychological and social factors which are central to the security (or not) of mental well-being. People with learning disabilities may have severely compromised attachment histories. Sinason (1992) has written eloquently about the traumatized response of a mother to her disabled child. In her shock, grief and shame she may be so caught up in her own strategies for survival that she is unable sufficiently to attend to the child about whom she may in any case be profoundly ambivalent, leaving the child with a sense of emotional abandonment and vulnerability. On the other hand, the mother may seek to overcome her feelings by being overprotective to the point at which the child is unable to find the space to develop as 'himself'. In both instances, the child may be unduly compliant and unprotesting, because of his fear of losing his attachment to his mother altogether. If, for whatever reason, primary maternal preoccupation continues for too long, an emotional dependency may emerge which leads to particular vulnerability when there is eventually a break in the relationship.

Many people with learning disabilities, especially those now in middle age, may have been in institutional care since childhood. They will have suffered a sudden and unexplained (or inexplicable) separation from their family of origin, and been required to live in an environment full of other people, but offering little chance of either lasting attachments or privacy. A constantly changing staff team with time to do little more than attend to physical needs and manage behaviour will have replaced parents. With so little opportunity for sustained intimacy there is no incentive to develop the capacity for emotional subtlety. Feelings are discharged in broad gestures often simply labelled as 'challenging' or in some other way identified as no more than part of a person's ordinary way of being, and are managed by physical, behavioural or pharmacological means. Many people in this age group have in recent years been returned to 'community' living. They have found themselves in new social and emotional circumstances in which there has been little opportunity to mourn the old life, however restricting, and in which their former defensive or regulatory strategies are no longer effective or acceptable.

Bowlby (1973) suggests that from our earliest experiences of relating we build what he called internal working models, which form our (largely unconscious) pattern for living. Although the earliest models are formed in infancy, they may be restructured or added to in later life in the light of more recent experience. The internal working model of someone with learning disabilities may be characterized by pessimistic assumptions about their limited value to others, the likelihood of recurring separations, their perception by others as a 'problem', and their own inability to be an agent of change. It is not surprising that someone with such a sense of themselves and of their place in the world, especially a world in which interpersonal understanding seems so uncertain and events, especially losses, so unpredictable, may be especially vulnerable to breakdown. A secure attachment functions as, amongst other things, a means of affect regulation. When we experience powerful feelings, especially of fear, we turn to our attachment figures. Without such security, overwhelming feelings may spill over into depression, anxiety and psychosis.

People with learning disabilities are also likely to be less resilient in the face of events that they experience as traumatic (Ryan 1994; McCarthy 2001). As Judith Herman remarks: 'Psychological trauma is an affliction of the powerless . . . traumatic events overwhelm the ordinary systems of care that give people a sense of control, connection and meaning' (Herman 1992: 33). 'The survivor is left with fundamental problems in basic trust, autonomy and initiative . . . the survivor's intimate relationships are driven by the hunger for protection and care and are haunted by the fear of abandonment and exploitation' (pp. 110–11). The incidence of post traumatic stress disorder (PTSD) in people with learning disabilities is something about which there is as yet little literature. McCarthy (2001) suggests that it may take many forms, including self-injury, obsessive behaviours, depression and behaviours associated with psychosis. Before PTSD began to be more widely identified in people with learning disabilities, the most common diagnosis was of schizophrenia.

The risk and prevalence of mental illness are significantly higher amongst people with learning disabilities than in the general population, but all are subject to the same range of disorders. Often the first reason for referral to specialist learning disability services, and to psychiatry or psychology in particular, is a change or disturbance in behaviour. This is of value up to a point: such disturbances may be anxious responses to environmental factors such as communication barriers, personal loss, or physical illness – or they may indicate a more significant deterioration in mental health. But these changes, although they alert professionals to difficulties, may not of themselves be helpful in more precise diagnosis. Phenomena such as self-injury, withdrawal or aggression may be part of the presentation in a range of psychiatric disorders.

Diagnosis may not be straightforward (Cooper 2003). Schizophrenia may be difficult to identify in someone who is already solitary and withdrawn, and its symptoms may be less florid than in someone with greater verbal ability. It may be difficult to distinguish schizophrenia from some presentations of Asperger's syndrome. Affective disorders such as depression similarly call for careful diagnosis and for thorough investigation of childhood problems, family history and any changes in present circumstances. Symptoms of anxiety may be seen as no more than ordinary responses to change, but the combination of potentially higher than ordinary stress factors together with limited coping strategies may lead to the development of significant anxiety disorders.

These difficulties in diagnosis can bring further problems. Whilst behavioural changes may be readily observable, their implications are not easy to interpret. As a result, there may be the risk of over-diagnosis; an example is schizophrenia, where 'strange' behaviours may be seen as indicators of psychosis, rather than of simple emotional distress. Equally, a treatable psychiatric disorder may be overlooked because it manifests simply as an extension of existing behaviours associated with learning disability.

This brief account of historical developments and current issues indicates a cycle of complex debates, reflective of how difficult it seems to be for the learning disabled person to take his place in the wider world. Professional interest in the inner worlds and emotional states of people with learning disabilities has fluctuated, and hopes have risen and fallen about the possibility of effective clinical understanding and support. As a result, people with learning disabilities have been easily marginalized, not only in social and familial terms, but also in terms of their interest as subjects of research and their access to adequate clinical (including psychiatric) services (Smith 1999).

Music therapy

So what are the implications of all this for music therapists? Literature on music therapy in psychiatry in Britain and Europe reveals a range of approaches. Some authors working in general psychiatry describe methods tailored to the particular diagnosis and resulting needs of the patient (Jensen 1999; Nygaard Pederson 2002). Others incline more to a psycho-dynamic model, taking account of the characteristics and difficulties inherent in a person's condition, but focusing primarily upon the conduct of the therapeutic relationship and the unfolding of unconscious processes (Woodcock 1987; John 1992).

Improvised music offers a non-verbal medium through which we may hope for more immediately intuitive, unconscious communication. Music therapists have found it useful to draw upon the work of Stern (1985) and Trevarthen (1993) in their investigations of the quality of early mother–infant interactions and their discussions of them in musical terms. This serves as a reminder that in music therapy we may be able to look beyond the immediate phenomena of symptoms, behaviour or diagnosis, and seek to engage on a level closer to the roots of emotional distress.

Recovery from illness, especially when it has been pervasive and long lasting, is itself a developmental task. However painful symptoms may have been, to move away from them is to experience oneself and the world in unfamiliar ways. Work in music therapy can offer the companionship and containment necessary for the negotiation of such a process. Other clini-cians may look for signs of returning 'normality' as indications of recovery. It may be in music therapy, however, that the patient can freely develop an idiosyncratic sound world (in itself a sign of greater creative energy) to reflect and manage the process of change. By bringing elements of the patient's music into a context in which they take their place in the overall structure of an improvisation, we acknowledge their significance and potential meaning. The music therapy room may be the first 'testing ground' for new experience. Most importantly, it may be the place where some of the dilemmas about aetiology and diagnosis discussed earlier in this chapter can hold a less prominent place in the therapist's thinking, and phenomena can be received as articulations (not necessarily translatable) of the patient's inner world. At the same time, the therapist needs to be well informed about all the current clinical thinking about the patient, and be aware of the impact and possible side effects of medication.

It is a common enough view in psychoanalytic work that therapy can only really begin at the point at which the patient can take himself seriously. Fonagy (2001) emphasizes the importance of 'mentalizing' in early development. If the caregiver can contain and give back to the baby something of his mental state, the baby is likely to develop with a more secure sense of contact with his own feelings, with the assurance that his experience merits serious attention. For people with learning disabilities, the experience of such a contained, worthwhile 'self' may have been much less available. Compounded by the inner disturbance and fragmentation of mental illness, any sense of a coherent self may be lost. Through her improvised responses the music therapist may come to be the imaginative, mentalizing 'other', drawing the patient's fragmented self into a musical relationship, and experiencing his gestures as meaningful.

Clinical material

The two case studies that follow are illustrative of some of the dilemmas and issues that may characterize work with people in this client group. Both took place with patients referred to the multidisciplinary team of which I am a member; names have been changed in order to preserve confidentiality.

Harriet

Harriet has a moderate learning disability. She was the youngest child of a large family in which both parents had had multiple partnerships and in which many of the children were step- or half-siblings. She grew up in a household in which sexual boundaries were not clear. Her own sexual initiation took place at the hands of a family friend when she was 13. She continued to be available to men both within and outside the family throughout her teenage years, and now believes that she suffered a miscarriage at the age of 15. Other family members, although chaotic in their private relationships, appeared to the outside world to be ordinary and successful. It fell to Harriet to hold the disorder and shame. She was the only visible sign (through her disability) of any family 'oddness', but was required to keep the secret.

When Harriet was 20 she got married to the son of neighbours. Her husband was violent and verbally abusive. She quite soon became pregnant. Feelings of excitement were mixed with fears that the baby would be a 'monster'. In the event, the baby was stillborn; it died in the womb and Harriet had to deliver a dead child. She was not shown her baby and does not know its sex or where it is buried. Shortly afterwards, her husband left her. In subsequent years Harriet had a succession of psychotic breakdowns, which led to repeated admissions to hospital. At various times she was cutting herself, talking of suicide, and hearing voices, especially that of her stepfather telling her that she was 'dirty'.

Harriet has an apparently wide vocabulary, but uses it without much flexibility. Clinical notes from that period (written by a long succession of doctors) suggest recurring frustration at her constantly repeated phrases and formulae. She received a diagnosis of schizophrenia and was prescribed medication and one course of ECT. Her learning disability was noted and some of her 'obsessive' behaviours were ascribed to it.

During one of her spells in hospital Harriet met her present partner, Andy. They have lived together for four years. At first things went well, not least because in attending to Andy in his recurring depressive episodes Harriet could take a responsible, caring position. As she began to think once again, however, about the prospect of having a baby, her voices and self-destructive impulses began to return. A new GP referred her to the learning disabilities team. The clinicians involved were the consultant psychiatrist, a community nurse and the music therapist. The referral to music therapy implied the recognition that a long-term therapeutic relationship might offer Harriet the opportunity to work through some of the profoundly traumatic events of her life. It also acknowledged that language, although available to Harriet, was a source of great anxiety to her.

Harriet's treatment within a team enabled different aspects of her experience to be attended to. The psychiatrist considered diagnostic possibilities and frequently reviewed her medication, keeping it as low as possible. The community nurse visited Harriet and Andy at home, to monitor Harriet's mental state and to support the couple through fluctuations in their relationship. Both of these interventions provided necessary containment for Harriet as she embarked upon therapy.

In the early stages of our work, Harriet seemed unremittingly positive towards me. She was complimentary about everything, while at the same time looking cautiously round the room and appearing very alert to any sounds from outside. We played calm, gentle, repetitive music on resonant metallophones. If I tried to introduce something a little more disruptive, she stopped at once and said 'It's going wrong' or sometimes 'I've gone wrong.' At first, the music served to create a degree of security between us and in the room. Harriet gradually became more engaged in it and less preoccupied with events outside. As the sessions went on, though, I had the sense that the music was being required to maintain a cover over something else. During these early sessions we spoke very little. Our exchanges were confined to practicalities and Harriet often ended one of her rather stereotypical sentences with 'and am I making sense?' It struck me that her fear of not making sense was very acute. In the past it had brought her into contact with her husband's violent attacks, and later taken her into hospital.

One week she chose a different beater, which produced a sharp clanging sound on the metallophone. She was at first shocked and then intrigued by the discovery that she could not only play more fiercely and loudly, but that she could apparently drown me out. She developed a rather raucous laugh that often accompanied her clanging playing, and at times she shouted 'Stop it!' as she chaotically struck the metallophone. It emerged that she was hearing the voice of her stepfather, telling her to cut herself, but now she seemed to be turning that energy towards an attack on the music and me. In the course of one of these frenzied outbursts she suddenly stopped playing and realized that my much quieter music was continuing. She began to cry.

In subsequent sessions two things happened: she began to talk more, but at the same time her language became more hesitant and fragmented. She gradually told the story of the loss of her baby and said, 'I wanted to hear him cry, like this.' She gave series of shouts and groans which I joined with on the piano, offering some containment for her grief. From that time onwards Harriet began to be able to recount more of her experience. When her feelings became too powerful for her, or the voice in her head began to intervene, she turned to the instruments, which she identified as a safe means of speaking and remembering because, as she said, 'In music we can start and stop.' Her control of the structure of the music (and of its idiom) offered a means of regulating her affective experience, enabling her to move through the process of grieving with less risk of falling into panic or into the fragmented mental states which had contributed to her diagnosis of schizophrenia. As she became more aware of her variable mental state, she was more able to monitor it. In one of our later sessions she asked me the question which forms the title of this chapter.

We worked together for two years, during which time the voices receded and her self-injury gradually stopped. Her personal boundaries grew stronger. She became more able to withstand some of Andy's incessant demands for care and attention, and better able to control her spending and her consumption of food. This was the first time Harriet had been offered long-term therapy. In the music we were able to 'hold' her experience sufficiently to enable her to work through her trauma at a manageable pace. It was essential that this work took place in the context of a multidisciplinary approach. It enabled the clinicians involved to draw upon one another's experience and sustain one another's capacity for thinking in the face of Harriet's projections and sometimes baffling communications. It also modelled for Harriet the possibility of a consistent 'family' in which the need for secrecy was replaced by communicative interest and concern, towards both her and one another.

Ben

Ben is now middle aged; he has severe learning disabilities. He was the youngest of seven children (the pregnancy was unwelcome) and from the beginning of his life his mother found his existence very hard to bear. In infancy he cried and could not be comforted; he often refused food and was seriously underweight. Early on he developed some of the self-harming behaviours that remained characteristic of him in adult life, particularly striking his head and hands on hard surfaces. There are entries in his notes that show that his mother could not discuss him with professionals without breaking down. His father is simply recorded as saying: 'Ben was never one of us.' There is some evidence that he was left alone for long periods. When he was four years old Ben was removed from the family home to a long-stay institution; from then on he gradually lost contact with his family. For the next 40 years he lived in various units with shifting populations of residents and staff.

At the time that he was referred to music therapy he was living on a ward with 12 other men, most of whom were more mobile and more aggressive than him. His self-injuring behaviour was always present, and at times he smeared himself and his surroundings with food and faeces. He was cared for by a staff team who were necessarily preoccupied with attending to other people and whose exchanges with him were limited to practical necessities (food, washing) or to intervening to try to prevent his self-damage. For many years he had been taking a powerful sedative medication on a daily basis and was addicted to it. He had no speech, though he was sometimes very vocal, and he had a wound which was often open and infected through his repeated head banging. He also had substantial damage to his right hand and was at risk of losing the sight of one eye.

The ward staff greeted the news of Ben's referral to music therapy with resignation and indicated that there was little point in it; that he had seen countless clinicians over the years, and that he was too disabled to be able to respond to anything. Perhaps in defensive reaction to his disturbing, baffling behaviour, and his intense difficulty in engaging in any communication that others experienced as meaningful, the professionals had resorted to a very fixed view of him which ascribed his behaviour to his extreme disability and thus categorized it as something to be managed at best, and survived at worst.

A new consultant psychiatrist was appointed who set about reviewing Ben with fresh eyes. She established a small team (psychiatry, nursing, music therapy and psychology) who would work with Ben intensively and colla-boratively, seeking new ways to think about his difficulties. In the security of this clinical group it became more possible to contemplate Ben's behaviours not necessarily as the fixed phenomena of disability, but rather as strategies of self-regulation and articulations of distress. It was proposed that Ben should gradually come off his current medication, with the risk that in the course of this his self-injury might become worse. At times it did, but it also allowed Ben to be more alert and steady on his feet, and more active in his responses to others. The process took three years. The psychiatrist suggested that some of Ben's features, including his low response to stimuli, his lack of interest in food and his difficulty in relating actively to other people might be read as signs of a depressive illness. She began treatment with antidepressant medication.

Throughout this period Ben was in weekly music therapy. In the early months his behaviour was very much as it was on the ward. He rocked restlessly, looked for opportunities for self-harm and ignored or rejected my offers of instruments. At that time there was little music other than what I improvised, trying to reflect something of my experience of being with him. We both sat on the floor. Ben often looked at his feet, but was increasingly watchful of any movements I made around the room. I marked the start and end of the session with the same sounds each week, using a gato drum. Initially Ben reacted sharply, either pushing the drum away or rocking urgently. I persisted with gentle sounds and as he became more tolerant of them it became possible to begin to match his movements with the pace and intensity of my playing.

After a few months Ben began to look for the drum when he came into the room and to push it towards me, and my music assumed a simple recurring rhythmic pattern. He showed no interest in touching the drum himself, but watched the movement of the beater with increasing alertness. His movement and my playing created an opening routine that lasted throughout our work together. My intention in the early stages was to try and create something different from his life on the ward (and perhaps in early family life), where he tended to be ignored unless he was harming himself, in which case there was an immediate move to stop it. In the sessions I hoped to offer a more continuing, attentive presence, both musically and in my relative physical stillness. I began to play other small percussion instruments, returning regularly to the gato drum as a kind of 'refrain'. Ben never actively played an instrument, but increasingly he would take one from my hand and explore its tactile qualities before carefully handing it back to me. This passing to and fro of instruments began to feel like a dialogue, and through that I moved into wordless vocalizing. In due course Ben began to make sounds of his own as well, and we built up a repertoire of vocal exchanges in which there was an increasing variety in volume and intensity. He began to discern and respond to more subtle changes in activity or sound, and to resort less to broad repetitive gestures. This was mirrored by a new approach on the ward where he now had a small, consistent group of carers who sought more actively to engage him in practical activity. Regular supervision enabled them to feel more able to think imaginatively about the experiences underlying his self-injury and to think about ways in which he might be supported through his change of medication. Self-injury remains a source of familiar self-regulation for him at times of intense anxiety, but in the care of people who are seeking to think about the meaning of his behaviour and about what might support improvement in his mental health, he resorts to it less often and with less intensity.

Ben serves as an example of someone whose behaviours are apparently so intractable that they generate a level of anxiety and despair in professionals which may make more open thinking about mental illness difficult. In this context the work in music therapy was made possible by its place in a wider team-based scheme of treatment that allowed Ben's underlying depressive illness to be considered and treated.

Both Harriet and Ben illustrate the difficulty in diagnosis presented by people with learning disabilities. In Harriet's case, her traumatic history was known, but she was initially treated in an acute general psychiatric service in which there was no provision for long-term therapy. In Ben's case, his behaviours were so extreme and his disability so severe that it had been difficult for a fluctuating staff team to work with anything beyond the immediate problems.

Music therapy within multidisciplinary practice

This is complex and demanding work. A well-functioning multidisciplinary team can model for its members, and thus for its patients, the possibility of integrated, active thinking. Within the team it may be the music therapist who can most readily hold the position of 'not knowing', represented by the improvisatory spirit of the music, and yet point to elements in the unfolding musical relationship which indicate change and integration. At the same time the music therapist needs to be well informed as to the implications of different diagnoses, and to understand the potential side effects of medication and the implications of medication changes. People with complex needs are at risk of that complexity being reflected in fragmented clinical treatment, with psychiatrist, psychologist, dietician and social worker, for instance, each attending to a particular area of concern, but in insufficient communication and debate with one another. There is a danger of music therapy also becoming part of that unsatisfactory pattern, especially if the music therapist senses (or fears) that an intuitive, psychodynamically informed approach may be at odds with the more clear-cut, goal-oriented practice of other clinicians. Good supervision is essential to provide a holding and thinking space for the anxieties and uncertainties inherent in the clinical work. It may also support the therapist in taking her place in the team and in finding a way to report upon clinical events in terms that do justice to the work, are accessible to colleagues, and so contribute to an integrated service for the patient.

As the early part of this chapter has outlined, people with learning disabilities and mental illness face an unusual constellation of problems which continues, at times, to be a source of uncertainty and frustration to clinicians. Music therapy on a long-term basis offers a space to engage not only with immediate symptoms, but with whatever is being played out through them in terms of underlying experience of trauma or loss, and to find, through a mutually negotiated musical encounter, a means to work towards a more integrated and coherent self.

Chapter 6

Friendship and group work

Clare L. Fillingham

> If you don't have friends you don't have nothing!
> (Maggie)

People with learning disabilities can often experience difficulties in building and maintaining friendships and relationships, which can impact on overall quality of life. Within a socio-political framework, this chapter discusses the way in which group music therapy can enable individuals to develop their capacity to make and keep friends. The chapter covers four areas: friendships and quality of life, group theory, a music therapy group case study; and music therapy research.

Friendships and 'quality of life'

> People need people – for initial and continued survival, for social-ization, for the pursuit of satisfaction. No one – neither the dying, nor the outcast, nor the mighty – transcends the need for human contact.
> (Yalom 1985: 23)

The valuable role that friendships and interpersonal relationships play in our lives is evident to most. As we advance through the different life stages, so our friendships and relationships evolve and shift, each one serving to shape and colour our existence in the world. The diversity of relationships throughout a lifetime can range from those within the family or social context to the more intimate, close friendships or sexual relationships we may experience outside it. It is within our network of friendships and relationships that we find social and emotional support, a counselling ear and another with whom to share opportunities and experiences. They allow us to feel valued and they help to define who we are (Firth and Rapley 1990). In whichever context, relationships play a vital role in our psycho-logical well-being and overall quality of life.

For many people with learning disabilities, however, a lack of friendships and an inability to form and sustain positive relationships is often a reality (Bayley 1997a; Sheppard 2003), the reasons for which can be wide ranging. An estimated 80 per cent of people with learning disabilities have some form of communication difficulties (Remington 1998), which will hinder the process of forming positive relationships. It is also well documented that this population often experiences difficulties in recognizing and expressing emotions (McKenzie *et al.* 2000). O'Connor focuses on personal identity, suggesting that a person may reject and devalue their peer relationships and that relationships with non-learning disabled people are more socially valued (2001: 304).

Firth and Rapley (1990) suggest that relationships can be difficult to establish and maintain due to practical, social, emotional and communication barriers, as well as acknowledging gender, class and culture differences that prevent positive relationships being established. They consider some of the conditions necessary to enable people to build friendships beyond acquaintance, which include:

- *Motivation: the desire to develop a relationship*
  The decision not to develop a relationship may be affected by other factors e.g. self-protection, past negative experiences of rejection, lack of self-confidence, self esteem.
- *Self-confidence: to establish, maintain and nurture relationships*
  This may be affected by past experience, physiological factors and is dependent on self-perception and others' perception.
- *Skills: intrapersonal and interpersonal*
  The ability to think about others, show empathy, to be able to make judgements on others' moods, attitudes and motivation, whilst having the skills to avoid or resolve conflict.
- *Opportunities: to explore relationships*
  To be able to learn, enhance and practice social skills.

(Firth and Rapley 1990: 59)

Sheppard (2003: 143) describes the rejecting relationships and poor role models that many people with learning disabilities have experienced in the past which may make it particularly difficult to form lasting relationships. She considers how a history of negative relationships may be relived through transference relationships, not only within group therapy but also with potential friends and she stresses the necessity for firm boundaries within therapy work. Outwith the context of group therapy, Bayley (1997a) considers the importance of firm structures in a person's life, to enable them to sustain and develop relationships. He emphasizes that those services which place a strong value on sustaining, nurturing and developing relationships need to commit considerable 'time, energy and resources' (Bayley 1997b: 30).

He argues that a learning disability is a lifelong diagnosis, and for this reason people have a continuing need for ongoing support to enable them to maintain positive relationships. Finally, it is suggested, in spite of limited evidence on the subject, that loneliness and the subsequent feelings of helplessness are significant factors in the aetiology of depression for people with learning disabilities (Prasher 1999). This evidence raises questions about the quality of life of learning disabled adults living in the community today.

Quality of life and people with learning disabilities

Quality of life has remained an important overriding principle by which to improve the lives and services of people with learning disabilities (Schalock 1996: vii). How it is defined as a concept and measured has however remained an elusive challenge for those involved in providing services over the last 30 years. Felce and Perry (1994) suggest that quality of life could be considered an interaction between a person's lifestyle, their satisfaction with their lifestyle and their personal values and aspirations (1994: 5). They offer the following definition:

> Quality of life is defined as an overall general well-being which comprises objective descriptors and subjective evaluations of physical, material, social and emotional well-being together with the extent of personal development and purposeful activity all weighted by a personal set of values.
>
> (Felce and Perry 1994: 14)

Over the last quarter century radical service reform has helped to improve the overall quality of life of people with learning disabilities (see Chapter 1). The principle of normalization in the 1960s initiated a change in perception and awareness of how people should be allowed to live a normal lifestyle, comparative with mainstream society. As a consequence of this philosophical shift, the White Paper *Better Services for the Mentally Handicapped* (DHSS) was launched in 1971 and prompted the gradual closure of long-stay institutions. People were gradually moved into the community and increasing attention was given to quality of life and how services should be provided. One might then assume that over the years the physical, material and social needs of people with learning disabilities have been greatly improved. However, evidence suggests that whilst people living in the community have considerably more contacts, these tend to be with people who provide a service, such as shopkeepers or with other family members and staff (Firth and Rapley 1990; Sheppard 2003). Community living has therefore not necessarily led to an increase in a person's circle of close friendships. This raises a fundamental quality of life question – does increased physical presence in the community actually equate to meaningful social presence? May cautions against making such an assumption when he writes: 'Integration is not inclusion, and dispersal to the community does not necessarily put an end to segregation and isolation, or enhance quality of life. On the contrary, it can inhibit the development of a collective identity and encourage self-blame' (2001: 13). These issues are explored further in Chapter 7.

It has been suggested that in spite of the many positive changes in service provision, the emotional lives and emotional difficulties of people with learning disabilities have been largely neglected and that many people are living an isolated and lonely existence in the community (Arthur 2003). However, social inclusion remains a key objective for services and has been well documented in the more recent governmental reviews in Scotland and England.

Social inclusion and The Same as You?

The Same As You? (Scottish Executive 2001) is the first policy initiative in Scotland in over 20 years and it outlines the key services involved in supporting people with learning disabilities of all ages (there are parallels with *Valuing People*, the English White Paper; DOH 2001c, see Chapter 1). As well as examining social and healthcare services and discussing the relationship of these services to housing, education and employment, the review stresses the importance of social inclusion, meaning that people are entitled to lead a full life, to feel valued and to be included in society (Scottish Executive 2001: 2). One of the key recommendations highlights the need for the major organizations involved in providing services to develop new ways of supporting individuals in order to achieve this social inclusion: 'Local authorities and health boards should both examine what they provide and develop more modern, flexible and responsive service which support people in the community through employment, lifelong learning and getting them involved socially' (2001: 97).

Whilst social inclusion is a fundamental objective there remains the question as to how this can be achieved in a meaningful way for the individual in view of the difficulties that people with learning disabilities can experience in forming and maintaining relationships.

An overview of group theory

Human living has always been in groups.

(Foulkes 1986: 23)

Much has been written on group therapy and the various approaches that have been developed (Bion 1961; Foulkes 1986; Pines 1983; Stock Whitaker 2001; Yalom 1985). Regardless of the type of group described, it is acknowledged that individuals will bring their own existing models of relating to the group; that unconscious processes will be at play; and that all groups will progress through different stages of development. Stock Whitaker (2001) provides a comprehensive overview of the diverse ways in which groups of people, who might benefit from a group experience, can be categorized. Inevitably the needs of the individual will determine the type of group that will be most appropriate.

Historically, therapeutic approaches for people with learning disabilities have focused predominantly on psychological theories of learning (Collins 1999). However, increasing attention has been given to undertaking analytical group psychotherapy with people with intellectual impairment as a way of exploring their emotional lives (Hollins and Evered 1990; Jones and Bonnar 1996; O'Connor 2001; Pantlin 1985). At the heart of psychoanalytically informed approaches is the belief that emotional communication is not dependent on verbal or cognitive ability (Hodges 2003; Sinason 1992; Watson 2002), which Lapping (2003) expands on in her detailed examination of the perception of emotional expression in music therapy with people who have a severe learning disability. It is thought that the analytic group setting can allow people to practise being with others (Jones 1996) and can help them to identify, understand and express emotions (O'Connor 2001).

Group analytic psychotherapy is a method developed by Foulkes in the 1940s. Through his extensive experience working as a psychoanalyst, Foulkes began to recognize the great potential for offering therapy in the context of a group, believing that 'social and environmental issues are as formative as internal emotional experience on the child's psychological development' (Barnes et al. 1999: 23). Foulkes writes that 'the mental health of the individual is dependent on his community' (Foulkes and Anthony 1984: 31). It is stated that communication is central to his theory, not only in terms of 'the mechanism of belonging' and 'the glue that holds the group together' (Dalal 2002: 112), but also that psychological illness is considered a 'malfunction in the communicational field' (2002: 112).

Foulkes's concept of the matrix provides a way of thinking about the complex network of communications and many layers of relationships that occur within the group. In contrast to other methods, Foulkes saw the group itself as the agent of change and therefore adopted the term group conductor, rather than leader, to denote the role of the therapist. The role of the conductor was to enable and empower the group to do its work (Chazan 2001) and to observe what was happening for the individual, whilst maintaining an overview of what was happening in the group as a whole. In thinking about the central tenet of this chapter, Foulkes offers the following pertinent thought: 'being a respected and effective member of the group, being accepted, being able to share, to participate, belong to the basic constructive experiences in human life' (Foulkes and Anthony 1984: 27).

The staging of the group and the boundaries that are established are essential to the group process. Concepts such as the holding environment

(Winnicott 1974), the secure base (Bowlby 1988) and containment (Bion 1961) are helpful in understanding particular properties of the therapy group: 'the outer predictability in terms of a setting, a set time and place can lead to an inner sense of being held in a safe place' (Barnes *et al.* 1999: 29). Dynamic administration is a term used in group analysis to describe all aspects of establishing a group. The conductor is required not only to consider the actual group, its composition and its boundaries, but must also take into consideration the setting and the organization within which the work will be undertaken, so as to minimize any potential disruptions to the group process.

Yalom's description of the formative early stages of group development is helpful in understanding the way in which a new group can evolve. He describes an initial period of orientation, where members search for goals and are dependent on the therapist for guidance and reassurance, followed by a period of conflict between members or members and therapist, shifting to a period of increased morale and mutual trust (1985: 299–313). He suggests that when the group has survived these early stages and achieved a sense of stability then it can begin the long working process (1985: 333).

Psychodynamic and group analytic theory have greatly influenced music therapy practice in Britain over the years. Davies and Richards provide a much needed addition to the music therapy literature on group work, which draws on strands of analytic theory from over the last century and includes contributions from music therapists working across diverse settings (2002). The book highlights the many ways in which music therapy in the group setting can help people to 'have an enriched experience, expressive as well as receptive, of themselves and others' (2002: 23) and allows conscious and unconscious aspects of the group process 'to be made audible' (p. 19).

In her recent paper on group work, Watson considers how a group can provide opportunities for people with learning disabilities to explore a way of being together which isn't reliant on words. She suggests that the music therapy group can provide opportunities for people to develop the skills and experiences necessary 'to integrate more fully into their wider groups and communities', drawing on Foulkes's thinking that a group 'starts a process of acceptance, sharing, participation and belonging' (Watson 2005: 1–2). This resonates with Yalom's (1985) idea of group cohesiveness, which he considers to be a precondition of effective therapy. He says that the highly cohesive group will impact positively on the commitment shown by members and will provide stability, allowing members to take risks and to begin to express conflict.

Clinical example – music therapy group

The following music therapy group was part of a research study, which examined how group music therapy might help to address some of the issues for people with mild-moderate learning disabilities who experience relationship difficulties. Six people (aged 30–50 years) with a learning disability (IQ 55–70) were selected to take part in the group. The sessions took place in a private music room at a local day centre and were facilitated by the author and a clinical psychologist from the team.

The group members

Alison is described as a sociable person, but she experiences considerable difficulties in maintaining her valued relationships. Following a past incident at the day centre, Alison and another participant (Catherine) have experienced a volatile relationship, which has resulted in staff changing the days that they both attend.

Beth is also described as being sociable, although she does not have many apparent close friends and she does not enjoy living with other people in her house.

Catherine has had extensive input from services owing to her lifelong difficulties with relationships and controlling her emotions. She was adopted as a baby and lived with her adoptive parents until she moved into her own flat.

David lives with his parents and enjoys a full and active life, focused mainly around sporting activities. Although David has a number of friends, he has difficulties in engaging in two-way interaction and therefore in maintaining positive relationships.

Jean has a long history of severe depression, aggressive behaviour and poor self-image due to her weight difficulties. Her mood swings and aggression have affected her ability to maintain positive relationships. Jean was taken into care at an early age and she was admitted to a learning disability hospital in her late teens. She now lives in supported accommodation.

Maggie has a recurrent depressive disorder and low self-esteem, which affects what she does and how she interacts with others. She has had ongoing difficulties with relationships over the years and she experiences frustration as a result of her inability to express in words how she feels.

Overview of the group

In the week prior to the start of the group there had been an incident between Alison and Catherine at college. This resulted in a sense of heightened anxiety and tension amongst the members in the first session. The group members hardly spoke to or looked at each other and they were very reliant on the therapists to initiate the interaction and to take charge. The music throughout the session sounded busy and disjointed, with a sense of members doing their own thing. Both David and Jean played at a quick pace on the drums and seemed to want to please the therapists with their music. Catherine's playing was quiet and tentative, whilst Beth looked out of the window, not seeming to attend to either her own or the group's playing. Alison offered a quiet but steady heartbeat pulse, which she maintained until the end of the piece. By the end of the session both Alison and Catherine seemed on the brink of tears.

During the early sessions the group remained heavily dependent on the therapists for the playing and talking, although there were spurious attempts by members seemingly wanting to make everything all right and to please. Comments were made such as 'we should all be friends in the group!' and topics of conversation often turned to safe non-group related themes such as the weather or bus timetables. However, Alison's dramatic entrance to the eighth session, where she announced angrily that she was 'here under protest!' seemed to act as a catalyst for the subsequent expression of more difficult feelings in the group. Her comments about how angry she felt towards staff stirred up considerable anxiety and caused resentment amongst the other group members. The uneasy, dissonant quality to the group music seemed to convey the feeling of tension in the room at the time. During the improvisation Alison sat with her arms tightly folded and legs crossed. She kept her head turned away from Catherine and shut one eye, as if to block her out completely. Both David and Jean played in a quick-paced and frantic manner, as if to fill the space and to avoid any conflict. Catherine remained on the periphery of the group throughout the playing, shaking the maracas in a tentative way so that they were barely audible. When Alison left the session early, the other members quickly offered reassurance to the therapists, saying that they shouldn't get involved and 'not to listen' to her. However, it was after this session that members began to voice objections about the way in which other members behaved, such as 'Catherine is always doing it' (being suspended).

By the halfway stage the theme of friendships and fighting had become central to the sessions. Group members began to speak more openly about how fighting between people made them feel, and they were able to take more risks in terms of addressing other members directly rather than indirectly or through the therapists. A significant moment was when Maggie raised the issue of Catherine and Alison's relationship in front of the whole group. She talked about how people falling out impacts on everyone and said that the group 'should be like a team'. She then turned to Alison and said, 'You and Catherine should be friends'. In view of the considerable anxiety that this relationship evoked amongst staff, Maggie's actions seemed particularly significant and marked a further shift in the group process.

In the latter stages of the therapy there was an increased sense of humour and playfulness in the group interaction. Another striking feature was the way in which members encouraged each other to take the lead in the music or offered praise and support. This was most evident in session 16 when Catherine returned to the group after a substantial period of absence and was encouraged by the group members to take the lead in the group improvisation. Catherine made a hesitant start, offering a moderately paced, quiet pulse, which the rest of the group immediately adjusted to. As the music evolved, most of the others watched her carefully and continued to match the speed and dynamic of her playing. Alison was sitting opposite Catherine and she maintained an open body posture throughout. At the end of the piece the members were quick to offer praise: 'I think she did really well!'. They asked her how she had felt about leading the group. Towards the end of this session there was a lively improvisation in which everyone seemed able to have a voice and to be heard. In contrast to the early improvisations, the music had a greater sense of cohesion and seemed to reflect the way in which the members had become increasingly sensitive and tuned in to each other's playing.

Commentary

Over the course of the 20 weeks the patterns of relating shifted constantly within the music and the talking. The volatile relationship between Alison and Catherine remained a focal point for the group throughout the sessions and may in some ways have provided other group members with a scapegoat, a phenomenon which Anthony says can be a regular feature of groups – a person 'upon whom the group can project all its accumulated guilty feelings' (Foulkes and Anthony 1984: 156). It was also apparent that there were issues and anxieties around authority, demonstrated in the responses of some of the members to the verbal attacks directed towards the staff and the therapists during the sessions. A striking feature of the group was that in spite of the turbulent relationship between Alison and Catherine each member showed great commitment. Alison, who had been threatened by Catherine on a number of occasions whilst the group ran, had the most consistent attendance. Catherine, who had been the instigator of the threats, had requested coming to the final session despite having been excluded from the centre at that time, owing to her ongoing difficulties.

As well as providing a secure base, the group seemed to provide opportunities for the members to explore components inherent in the relationship-building process in terms of motivation, self-confidence and interpersonal/intrapersonal skills (Firth and Rapley 1990). Maggie's statement that the group should be like a team on the one hand resonated with the idea of group cohesiveness (Yalom 1985). However, an alternative interpretation of the team might be around the group needing a common purpose – a sense of needing to stick together. Having a learning disability was something that linked each member of the group, but was never openly discussed in the short period that the group ran.

Music therapy research: relationships and quality of life

Methodology

A collective case study design within a qualitative framework was used to explore relationship difficulties in this music therapy group (Fillingham 2003). The study was placed in the context of quality of life to consider the wider impact of music therapy intervention. In order to look at changing patterns of relating in the group, changes in the level of *musical connection* in the group's improvisational play were rated. The study also examined the ways in which events in the group and perception of quality of life of the participants were linked.

The six participants were selected to take part in the group by the day centre manager. A semi-structured interview based on O'Brien's five accomplishments (1992) – relationships, competence, respect, community presence and choice – was undertaken by a speech therapist with each participant, their key worker at the centre and a member of residential staff, before the group began and on its completion. The interview was used to gain insight into each person's own thoughts and feelings on relationships and quality of life issues and to provide a before-and-after measure. To measure the changes in the level of musical connection a simple coding system was developed. This had four categories, defining the degrees of connection within the group music (minimal, low, medium and high). Two music therapists independent of the research were shown four eight-minute video extracts in random order. They were asked to rate the degree of musical connection at 30-second intervals and were given musical criteria to assist them in their decision making (e.g. are there shared rhythms, shared beats? Does the music sound fragmented or cohesive?).

Results

Interviews – five accomplishments

RELATIONSHIPS

The responses to the first two interview questions (name your friends and who is your best friend?) demonstrate that friends named were mostly other service users at the day centre or staff (see Tables 6.1 and 6.2). None of the participants mentioned friends outwith the day centre. Key workers and residential staff also gave their opinions on this question, but for the purposes of this chapter only the participants' responses are reported. Table 6.3 presents additional comments that were made during the interview, which further highlight the impoverished nature of the relationships experienced by most of the participants.

When asked why friends are important, the participants tended to offer practical responses rather than emotional or personal responses: for

Table 6.1 Pre-therapy interview – Question 1: Name your friends

Names given	Alison	Beth	Catherine	David	Jean	Maggie
Service user	XXXX	X		XXXX	XX	
Staff member			X		XXXXX	XX
Social worker						
Family member			X			
Friend at home						

X = one person
0 = one person in the music therapy group

Table 6.2 Pre-therapy interview – Question 2: Who is your best friend?

Names given	Alison	Beth	Catherine	David	Jean	Maggie
Service user	XXXX	X			X	
Staff member				X		X
Social worker						
Family member			X			
Friend at home						

X = one person
0 = one person in the music therapy group

Table 6.3 Comments made about friends during interviews

Catherine	'I haven't got many.' 'Don't have one.' (a best friend)
Catherine's key worker	'Catherine doesn't have any (friends), staff who work with her; previously had friends but rejected a lot.'
Catherine's social worker	'Catherine has no friends – sees staff as friends.'
Beth's home leader	'Beth relates to staff rather than tenants.'
David's key worker	'David has love–hate relationships.'
Jean's key worker	'Jean talks a lot, but (they're) not friends.'
Maggie's home leader	'Maggie has no friends as such.'
Maggie's interviewer	'Maggie has no sense of closeness/quality from her relationships.'

example, 'go out and do things with them'. The responses to the questions around what is good about having friends and what you might do with them were mixed. The key activities mentioned included socializing such as going out (to the pub, shops, cinema, on walks). The responses highlighted that whilst participants undertook a lot of activity in the community, they generally went out on their own or with members of staff.

COMPETENCE, COMMUNITY PRESENCE, CHOICE, RESPECT

The responses for the remaining questions provided further valuable information on the lifestyles of each of the participants. Feedback from questions on competence centred around activities in the home (cooking, housework)

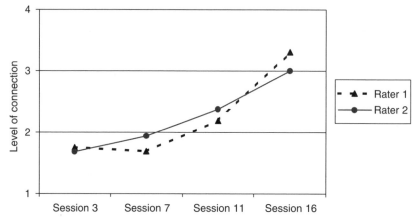

Figure 6.1 Mean level of connection across sessions

or at the day centre (gardening group, doing jigsaws). There was occasional reference to community-based activity, such as going to the cinema or swimming. Although there was a lot of community activity or presence, it was apparent that the participants were generally on their own or with key workers. Reference was made to the fact that a person's disability seemed to restrict the level of choice, for example, the ability to go on holiday independently. To the questions on respect (Have people been nice to you this week?) there were significant differences across the three groups and it was apparent from a number of staff responses that the participants' mood affected how other people interacted with them (e.g. 'It depends on how she feels'. 'She can be bossy'. 'She feels others don't like her'.). At the end of the interviews, the participants were asked about their overall quality of life at that time. Whilst each person said that they generally felt happy, the staff reported that there were issues, such as relationship problems, which they felt affected the participants' overall happiness and well-being.

MUSICAL DATA – LEVEL OF CONNECTION

Figure 6.1 demonstrates the results of the coding undertaken by the raters. The graph demonstrates a clear shift in the *level of musical connection* within the group over the course of therapy (1 = minimal, 2 = low, 3 = medium, 4 = high).

POST-THERAPY INTERVIEWS

In the post-therapy interview there were a number of changes in responses to the first two questions as shown in Tables 6.4 and 6.5. Three of the participants named at least one other group member as being a friend,

Table 6.4 Post-therapy interview – Question 1: Name your friends

Names given	Alison	Beth	Catherine	David	Jean	Maggie
Service user	XXX0	X		000	XXXXX	XX000
Staff member			XX		XX	X
Social worker						
Family member						
Friend at home						

X = one person
0 = one person in the music therapy group

Table 6.5 Post-therapy interview – Question 2: Who is your best friend?

Names given	Alison	Beth	Catherine	David	Jean	Maggie
Service user	XX	X			X	0
Staff member			X	X		
Social worker						
Family member						
Friend at home						

X = one person
0 = one person in the music therapy group

which in two instances was supported by a key worker. Jean named more service users than staff, and Maggie, who had given the names of two staff in the first interview, now named five service users as being friends. The key workers for Jean and David named an additional service user during the second interview. In terms of a best friend, Maggie named another group member during the second interview and Catherine, who had previously said she had no best friend, now named a member of staff.

Discussion and conclusion

These results might suggest common ground between the music therapy process and aspects of friendship development. Whilst making friends might not be an anticipated ideal outcome of therapy, as this would seem to perpetuate the problem of limited friendship opportunities, the music therapy group could be seen to provide a space in which conditions necessary to build friendships (Firth and Rapley 1990) can be explored. For example, the data showed that most participants did place value on friendships and were committed to the group, which suggests that motivation to relate to others was present. The increase in the level of connection in the group music might indicate that self-confidence in relating to others and to the instruments was increased and that interpersonal skills (tuning in to the quality of others' playing and offering encouragement and praise) were enhanced. The way in which the participants became more able to challenge each other directly and to take risks also suggests a notable increase in both self-confidence and the ability to deal with conflict.

In view of the natural context of the study it would be difficult to postulate that the changes in the interview responses were directly attributable to the music therapy intervention. However, the study did demonstrate the potential for offering music therapy in a group setting to enable people to explore different patterns of relating. The fact that certain participants remained unable to talk to or look at each other during the sessions made the results of the musical coding particularly significant. It seemed that within the containment of the therapeutic environment the music enabled people to be together and to explore positive and creative ways of relating to each other, as well as providing opportunities for each individual to explore an alternative means of emotional expression. Whilst the short life of the group meant that it was not possible to address deeper underlying issues, it had achieved a degree of stability and had begun a process of acceptance, sharing and belonging (Foulkes and Anthony 1984: 27). It might therefore be conjectured that the group was perhaps ready to begin the 'long working process' (Yalom 1985: 333). By placing the study within the framework of quality of life it was possible to think about the therapy, the participants and the issues they face in a broader, more holistic way. The interviews provided the participants with a voice and highlighted just some of the difficulties and challenges facing vulnerable people and marginalized groups living in the community today.

In summary, this chapter draws attention to the very real challenge of social inclusion. At a fundamental level many people with learning disabilities may need assistance not only with basic skills in friendship building, almost as a precondition to relationships, but may also require ongoing social and emotional support in order to sustain them. Without helping people to first lay these foundations and then to build on them, there is a danger that social inclusion and integration are rendered empty and meaningless concepts and that overall quality of life will be compromised. Whilst there are also wider societal issues and attitudes that need consideration and cannot be addressed by one profession alone, music therapists have a key role to play in enabling and empowering people to engage in society in a more active and meaningful way.

Acknowledgements

I would like to thank the service users who participated in the study and gave permission for their story to be told (names of participants have been changed to ensure anonymity and confidentiality), the day centre staff, my co-therapist Kirstin Sharp and my colleagues within the team for their continued support; and finally Kay Louise, whose memory has been a source of inspiration.

Chapter 7

Community, culture and group work

Tessa Watson

Community remains stubbornly missing, eludes our grasp or keeps falling apart, because the way in which this world prompts us to go about fulfilling our dreams of a secure life does not bring us closer to their fulfillment; instead of being mitigated, our insecurity grows as we go, and so we go on dreaming, trying, and failing.

(Bauman 2001: 44)

Community and culture

So much has been written about community in relation to healthcare trends that we may assume we know what the concept of community is. Terms such as care in the community and deinstitutionalization give a picture of community as being the environment outside an institution. However, there has been much sociological and political debate in recent years about a changing definition of community (Alperson 2002; Amit 2002; Bauman 2001; Eaton 2002; Gray 2002; Philipson *et al.* 2002; Shakespeare 1998), and it is useful to consider this here. Amit talks about community as being 'an idea or quality of sociality', going on to suggest that 'this thrust towards ideation has been associated with a translation of community as collective identity rather than interaction' (2002: 3). In the twenty-first century, community may be a sense of having something in common that could develop into social interaction, rather than a close knit, directly interacting network. Gray writes of this sense of togetherness as being a variety of shared experiences such as 'culture, location, occupation, interest, ethnicity, national identity' (2002: 40). A community may therefore exist in a country, neighbourhood, day centre, family, or group who share particular ideas or attitudes. This conceptualization perhaps conflicts with the particular meaning of care in the community in the UK.

Bauman questions the idea of community as being relevant to our times, writing of the difference between 'the community of our dreams and the "really existing community"'. He suggests that the new idea might be identity rather than community (2001: 4). So there may be an ideal of community that is rarely found:

> People who dream of community in the hope of finding a long-term security which they miss so painfully in their daily pursuits, and of liberating themselves from the irksome burden of ever new and always risky choices, will be sorely disappointed. Peace of mind, if they find it, will prove to be of the 'until further notice' kind. Rather than an island of 'natural understanding', a 'warm circle' where they can lay down their arms and stop fighting, the *really existing* community will feel like a besieged fortress being continuously bombarded by (often invisible) enemies outside while time and again being torn apart by discord within; ramparts and turrets will be the places where the seekers of communal warmth, homeliness and tranquility will have to spend most of their time.
>
> (Bauman 2001: 14)

People with learning disabilities have their own communities, both artificially and naturally constructed, and individuals may choose to live within these or not. Like all small communities, in order to take part in some of the activities of life people may need to come outside their community and engage with another.

Community and people with learning disabilities

> The truth is that living in the community is not a simple option. Families and individuals who have been doing it for countless years testify to the struggle against stereotyped attitudes and expectations, the exclusions and hurtfulness arising from ignorance and prejudice.
>
> (Brechin 1988: 112)

The idea of community may have particular meaning for people with learning disabilities, who through history have been allocated to an artificial community. Indeed, Ho states that the diagnosis of learning disability is 'a social construction that is highly contingent and reflects the medical and social attitudes of a particular society in a specific era' (2004: 89). When in the late 1960s and early 1970s there was a great change in sociology and a growth in the civil rights movement, Wolfensberger's concept of normalization (later renamed social role valorization) had an influence on services in the UK. This concept aims to use 'culturally valued means in order to enable, establish, and/or maintain valued social roles for people' (Wolfensberger and Tullman 2002: 139; see also Emerson 1992; Malin 1987). These significant changes in ideas prompted a move towards community-based services replacing institutions, with a great impact on people with learning disabilities, many of whom were living in hospitals or other large institution-like homes. Race documents the struggle to develop a coherent, clear path for services to follow in the 1980s and 1990s (Race 2002: Chapter 11). Whitehead considers issues around the loss of institutions and the move to community services:

> Outside in the new services, however, we continue recreating the splits which characterize our internal worlds, joining cliques which use certain techniques or jargon, or advocating a particular approach to the work. What is missing in the community is a replication of two vital functions of institutions: that of providing a repository for collective projections of madness and difference; and an organizational structure that contains the anxiety aroused by caring for people perceived to be different.
>
> (Whitehead 1992: 89)

Therefore we may consider that the wider community can offer new opportunities but is unable to provide some other functions of an institution. To take this further, O'Brien speaks of the importance of *real* integration for people with learning disabilities, describing it as follows: 'measures and practices that maximize community participation by using ordinary facilities as much as possible and by providing needed special services and restrictions in ways that are individualized to changing needs' (2005: 15). Communities, he suggests, can 'absorb and integrate' small numbers of different people, but may fight against larger numbers (p. 15). When a community is defensive, frightened or uninformed, it may react by imagining and speaking of risk. This can lead to sensationalist and inaccurate information and defensive attitudes as communities feel the need to protect themselves (the acronym NIMBY has emerged to describe this, standing for Not In My Back Yard). The building of resilient communities is described by Eliatamby and Hampton (2001) who consider that it can enable full citizenship or integration to be realized.

In the UK, the government white paper *Valuing People* recommended full access to community services, encouraging workers to assist people to 'lead full and purposeful lives within their community and to develop a range of friendships, activities and relationships' (2001c: 76). But some writers, including Klotz, are clear that we should not make people 'conform to normative social practice and behaviours as the means for their social inclusion and acceptance' (2004: 101). Despite community being a 'warmly persuasive word' (Mayo 2000: 37), there are difficulties in being part of a community if you are unable to communicate and interact in usual ways (McIntosh and Whittaker 1998). These same authors note that 'it is through sharing experiences that we make friends, have allies. We become more prepared to engage with the world outside' (McIntosh and Whittaker

2000: 32). There is a difficult balance to find between enabling people to use their communities independently and offering enough support to allow them to do this confidently and safely.

Bayley writes of real lives in the community, noting that 'the ultimate question is not "is this person well integrated into the community?" but "is this person happy?"' (1997b: 88; see also Firth and Rapley 1990; Sheppard 2003). He considers that integration for people with learning disabilities in a community is usually superficial, stating that people need to know what to do and how to make relationships once they have a place in a community. This is something that people with learning disabilities often have not been able to rehearse in a spontaneous and independent way. Szivos further notes that the geographical community is expected to provide networks of friendship, something that rarely happens in today's communities. Instead we 'rely upon the sophisticated use of travel and communications technology to maintain extended friendship and kinship networks' (1992: 118). The idea of normalization and real integration therefore remains a difficult issue in the twenty-first century as we support people with learning disabilities to find their place in their preferred community. As ideas about health and community change, it is important that we do not replace one rigid concept or belief with another, but that we continue to interrogate theory and practice. Chapter 6 in this book also considers these issues.

Music therapy, culture and community

In the foreword to the book *Culture Centred Music Therapy*, Bruscia speaks of the way in which new ideas are integrated into existing culture (2002: xvi). This is certainly true of music therapy which has seen dialogue between established and new models of practice. Holding in mind O'Brien's words 'absorb and integrate', this part of the chapter will consider ideas of culture and community in music therapy work, including the models of culture centred and community music therapy. A consideration of culture is essential when working as a therapist in order to be able to engage with the real world of the client. As Kenny and Stige state:

> When meeting a new client, the therapist should acknowledge that she or he is different from any other client in some respects, similar to some other clients in some respects, and like any other client in other respects. In other words: the person has a personal history, belongs to a cultural group, and is at the same time a human being sharing human nature with any other human being.
>
> (Kenny and Stige 2002: 22)

Stige also reminds us that 'meanings are always situated in cultural contexts' (2002: 49). The therapy that each music therapist offers will have a particular culture, and in each piece of clinical work this therapy culture meets the culture of the client. The therapist needs sensitivity and flexibility to work with the needs of each individual or group and this will inevitably lead us to ask, as Stige suggests, 'which theory? . . . for whom, when, and for what? . . . [and] how could we best use theory from other disciplines?' (2002: 35).

Another new model of music therapy, which has been titled community music therapy, exists to challenge conventional thinking (Ansdell 2002; Pavlicevic and Ansdell 2004). Community music therapy suggests that music therapy is a political or social concept that brings clients closer to music rather than a treatment that uses music to bring clients to greater health. An implied difference between this and other models seems to be that the main aim of community music therapists is to engage in cultural or community music making with the client, whereas other models of music therapy provide therapeutic support for clients' experience of their communities, promoting independence and allowing the sharing and processing of issues. Both ways of working hold at the centre the powerful and universal therapeutic action of music in life. Boal's idea of the theatre of the oppressed is interesting to compare here. This concept has grown from political oppression and has had an influence on the profession of dramatherapy. It describes a process-oriented creative system where issues are dealt with in drama; where people 'rehearse strategies for personal and social change' (Schutzman and Cohen-Cruz 1994: 1; and see Boal 1995).

Stige states that 'culture-centred music therapists sometimes take music therapy out of the music therapy room and out of the context of a session with a defined start and end' (2002: 43). We can read in other chapters in this book how music therapists carefully consider the culture and communities in which they work and what this means for their practice. Rhian Saville describes work that moves from the therapy room to the client's flat and back again (Chapter 3). The current author describes work in an adapted therapy room where the group is floor based (Chapter 8). Ben Saul writes of research that considered the way in which the culture or community of music therapy met that of carers (Chapter 9). I have written elsewhere of music and art therapy groups (a mix of communities/cultures) that moved from the therapy room to the community together. In these groups, our aim was to offer a therapeutic process. When the group visited the Tate Britain gallery, we experienced a different community together, and needed to be able to return to the containment of the therapy space to reflect on the experience (Watson and Vickers 2002).

Transdisciplinary working and project work are viewed by culture-centred and community music therapy as non-traditional music therapy roles. However, amongst music therapists working with people with learning disabilities there is a strong tradition of this work. Therapists might see the facilitation of community work, as well as diverse transdisciplinary projects as a part of their role (see Twyford and Watson, forthcoming). For example, as well as providing music therapy sessions the current author has taken on varied roles in music therapy work: arranging music workshops; going into the community with groups of clients; running joint groups with other professions in the wider day centre environment (see Chapter 10); and developing training for care staff.

The second part of this chapter describes a music therapy group that focused on community issues.

Music therapy groups focusing on community issues

I have run several groups specifically assembled to address issues around community life and the case study that follows is a composite illustration of several such groups. The challenges that our communities present for people with learning disabilities can be great. Alongside the everyday negotiations of community life, they may meet people and attitudes that are curious, tactless or cruel (as well as interested and generous). There are also significant barriers to communication with people and everyday services. In the groups described, music therapy has provided a place to share and reflect on painful and joyful issues of difference, disability, achievement and friendship through self-expression in music and talk. The aim of the therapy is always to encourage greater independence. Group music therapy allows people to come from their communities into a place of therapeutic safety in order to explore the difficulties in their lives, and to leave having shared these experiences positively, and perhaps having developed more skills to manage their lives.

Few authors have written about music therapy work that addresses issues of community life. Talking about their work with people with a formal diagnosis of mild learning disabilities, Richards and Hind state that 'for such people life is difficult in quite particular ways. They occupy an awkward middle ground. They are often not visibly or recognizably handicapped, but nor are they able to live independently' (2002: 120). In their writing, these therapists describe the importance of a secure base (Bowlby 1979) from which the group can 'begin to make discoveries on their own terms' (Richards and Hind 2002: 131). In the casework described below this was also the case. The group needed to establish their own music therapy community before they could begin to bring painful or joyful experiences to share and explore, before they could freely reveal parts of themselves normally kept hidden.

Recently, group psychotherapy work with people with learning disabilities has been documented, providing useful reflection on the issues in group work for this client group. Hollins and Evered write about working with 'disturbing conflicts' on issues of dependence and separation, feelings of not being wanted or of being a failure, and of improvement in social relationships (1990: 58). Jones and Bonnar (1996) note that issues of separation, loss, abandonment and rejection are evident, and that this can lead the group to take a long time to use other members as a source of support. This points to the need for a long-term, protected therapeutic space which can allow trust to develop.

'The community = think of all the things you really don't want to do – and then you have to do them' (group member)

The beginning of one music therapy group was prompted by changes in a day centre that meant members had greater opportunities to take part in community activities. This large centre developed a range of innovative outreach projects in the community and clients were invited to join some of these. It was noted that these opportunities caused considerable anxiety for some people, and a music therapy group was established to support these new experiences. Some of the experiences that the group aimed to explore were as follows:

- managing a new environment
- developing confidence
- meeting new people and developing social skills
- working as a team with others
- exploring identity and difference, coping with discrimination and prejudice
- coping with a sense of responsibility.

This group forms the basis of this case study, with examples from other groups used to illustrate further points.

Beginnings

It felt important at the start to explain the purpose of the group in a way that firmly linked the new community opportunities and the music therapy group. The group was described to potential group members in words and in Makaton signs and symbols as a place where people could bring and share their thoughts and feelings about experiences inside and outside the day centre. The group was described as a place of help if things were difficult; when people were scared or didn't want to leave the centre, or had difficulty being with others when they were in the community.

As with all groups, this group needed to find its own way at the beginning of the sessions. This process of forming involved a lot of thought from the therapists and the group members about what could happen in the sessions: about using the instruments, listening to each other, playing together, waiting, sharing, leading, listening; teamwork. From anxious beginnings where there was often silence and a reliance on the therapists, the musical medium allowed responsive and creative links to develop. As confidence and trust grew, the group became a place owned by the members, where concerns and joys were shared, and exciting and new things could happen. The real value of the group seemed to be its role as a place where feelings could be brought, spoken about or expressed. For some this may have been the only place they could bring deep and private feelings. That all feelings were allowed, valued and contained was of great importance.

The group members are invited to choose instruments. Growing from small, rhythmic sounds, the music becomes a lively, energetic group piece. The group members look around in excitement as the musical interactions develop between them, and singing and clapping adds to the group sound. The music feels purposeful and exciting, and lasts for a long time; new ideas adding to the texture and melody lines whenever the music begins to fade. When the piece ends there is clapping and laughter; we feel as though we have really worked together.

Confidence – having a voice and a place

The path from passivity to confidence was an important part of the group process in the first few months. The members were at first passive, reluctant or unable to use the group in their own way. They were encouraged to bring their own musical ideas, rhythms, phrases and ways of playing (modelled by the therapists). Gradually, individuals began to bring ideas, which were valued, and to realize their impact on the group. Verbal responses to the music were encouraged, as was discussion (for example: it's too loud, I like it – I don't like it, let's do it like this, that's sad, it's different for me). In our small music therapy community, ownership and confidence became possible, and this paralleled some of the processes taking place outside the group. However, we recognized that the difference between having confidence in a small, therapeutic group and owning a place in the community was great.

In one session, A says that the music is too loud and he will have to leave. He isolates himself from the group (as he often feels isolated in the community). We ask him how the music would need to change for him to be able to stay that day. A demonstrates some music and the other group members are able to listen and play with him. He has an idea, influences the group, changes things for himself and the group, and remains included.

Making relationships – what do we want, what do we need

The group returned to the theme of relationships many times. The whole range of relationships in life, such as those with family, friends, girlfriends/

boyfriends, husbands/wives, children and workers, were thought about in the group. Social skills were explored, with group members finding out how they could be together; how to make contact with new people, develop supportive friendships, and say goodbye when someone left. Events in the group and outside the group (including from the television and community) were used to think about these issues. Some difficult moments came when group members were not able to understand or communicate with each other verbally in the way in which they wanted. At these moments, the music was able to bridge some of the barriers to communication, allowing the group to feel close again.

An episode of the television soap EastEnders was described in the group, and from it came ideas: 'You could take someone with you to the pub like they do on EastEnders, you could take Patrick' (a group member). Whilst this seemed exciting for some, one person was frightened of the idea of himself or others going to the pub. These seemed to be brave explorations and following the discussion, feelings were expressed in quite chaotic, anxious music. The music was fast and loud, with singing and shouting of 'We'll go to the pub' and 'No! no!' from group members.

Alongside this exploration of relationships came expressions of the responsibility that group members felt when relationships ended or went wrong in some way. Some group members explored the difficulty, anger or shame that they felt when needing to ask for help from people (workers or family) and how they wanted to be able to support and help in return. Others described a sense of worry or responsibility that they had made things happen, 'Was it my fault that X left?', and also anxiety about whether they could manage to be an equal partner in a relationship.

Exploring inside and outside the group

As the group developed, we continued to link it closely to community experiences. Group themes that arose were discussed with the workers running the community project, although the explicit content of the group in relation to individuals was kept private. This ensured that useful feedback was gained and given. Sometimes artifacts from community visits were brought into the group to make a direct link with experiences. In particular, photographs were useful in making direct connections with experiences and associated feelings. Group members described their experiences in the community in very different terms, both positive and punitive (hence the title of this case study).

Visits to workplaces to think about different jobs were for some exciting and for others frightening. At times it was hard to hold these contrasting feelings and views in the group, and much of the anxiety that was felt due to these mixed feelings was expressed in our music. The members were, however, committed to supporting each other, and gradually developed an appreciation of each person being different and having different feelings and views. Allowing these different feelings to be expressed and managed in a group setting appeared to allow greater strength to grow within the group. The support between group members increased significantly, with people often providing ideas about what to do if someone was distressed (for example, the kind of comfort they might provide or music they might play to help the person):

Toby: We went to the police station, it was great! I really enjoyed it.
David: I didn't enjoy it, I fell over, I got upset [*becoming distressed*]. I don't want to go on trips, it makes me feel unhappy, I'm upset [*stands up, looks agitated*]. I'll have to leave . . .
Therapist: The visit was okay for some people and not for others. How can we help David, he's feeling worried?
John: David, you'll be alright. Let's play some music.

The group plays some calming, soft music, with David on the metallophone, his favourite instrument. He becomes calmer and begins to play assertively, looking around and nodding at the group. After the music has finished:

David: I feel better now, I like the music, it helps me to calm down. It's a good group.

The broadening of experiences in the community led to group members thinking about what they might want for themselves in the future – girlfriends, a job, a family. Some people were able to express their wishes and dreams in the group. Others reflected on the past with sadness and anger, remembering when some of these universal wishes were denied to people with learning disabilities (one group member remembered when he had worked but not been paid, and wanted a girlfriend but been discouraged). During the group several members joined a work project, and one group member talked about meeting a new girlfriend. This brought a sense of hopefulness for the future.

Community inside and outside the group – confronting disability and difference

Within the community of the group grew an exploration of difference. This included the awareness that some people talked more than others, or played more than others. These differences were sometimes seen as worrying, particularly if they raised conflict. A parallel process took place on community visits, where stark differences in ability were observed and experienced. In one session, an incident in the community was recounted, with one group member saying of another: 'He couldn't understand, because he's got a learning disability.' This led to the brave acknowledgement that each person in the group had a disability, which might make some things difficult. For some people this seemed helpful. It may have been the first time that they had spoken about their disability and difference to others. For others it provoked feelings of anger and unfairness. This theme was returned to several times, and our music played an essential role in containing some painful feelings around difference.

Gillian: I tried to use the till . . . [*in the shop where her brother works. There is a painful pause*] I couldn't, you know . . . it was too much for me. My brother says I can't use it again.

Andrew: I know, it's not fair. I want to be a doctor, giving out the tablets and telling people what's wrong. But I can't.

The music that follows this exchange is discordant and disconnected. Andrew plays loudly, desperately trying to lead the music, but not sure how. One of the therapists has to ask him to take care in case he breaks the drum. He shouts 'I'm ANGRY!'

After the music, Gillian talks about seeing the film *Evita*, and says that Evita was very powerful, but couldn't stop her own death. This thoughtful statement about power and powerlessness seems appropriate to the group.

Sometimes it was hard to accept difference within the group and the therapists were aware that a parallel process of discrimination could be transferred from the community to the therapy room. At times the therapists needed to protect group members from others who used their increased feelings of confidence and power to make an attack on someone they saw as more disabled than themselves (for example, to verbally attack a person who responded to schizophrenic symptoms in sessions, who found speaking difficult, or who could not read the words on the chart used to prepare for a break). The idea of projective identification was thought about in relation to these painful, attacking moments. Linked to this, a striking moment occurred when one of the members brought in a magazine article to show us. He had seen percussion instruments like those in the music therapy room in a photo accompanying an article about Evelyn Glennie. Discussion around this led to extreme interest that this world famous musician is profoundly deaf.

Inevitably the therapists experienced envy – of their roles as workers, their ability to play particular instruments and to manage the group. At times it was hard to tread the balance between the group having control of sessions and the therapists needing to provide structure or focus. In the music, these feelings of envy appeared to be expressed through bids for leadership of the group, often heard in the volume of the music.

Empowerment in endings – taking control and making decisions

As people moved on and new members joined the group two issues arose. First, existing group members had an experience of being helpful and supportive to new members, giving them confidence and a sense of validation. Second, the therapists became aware that several group members had no wish to move on and make changes in their lives. This could reflect ambivalence: boredom at a current situation, but a fear of moving on. It also represents a tension between the wishes of clients and the wishes of workers or organizations. How can we respond when clients reject opportunities for change? In this group the therapists felt that some members could not progress past a particular point of experience (and perhaps emotional defence).

The process of group members joining and leaving the group was linked by the therapists to people having their own ideas about when their therapy might be finished. Group members were given the opportunity to meet individually with the therapist to discuss this if they wished. Meeting, greeting and saying goodbye are intrinsic to all groups, but people with learning disabilities may not be used to having control over decisions to do with their joining or leaving day centres, jobs or communities (see Mattison and Pistrang 2004). In addition, some group members felt that others left because of something that they had done, and this seemed to reflect a deeply held anxiety about a capacity to damage others.

It was hoped that members could be empowered to make their own decisions (with the support of the therapist, and sometimes in discussion with staff or family members). Each person's leaving was given importance and prepared for. Accessible information was used to help the group prepare for goodbyes, and all were encouraged to share their feelings in relation to these endings. These feelings were expressed through music, speech and physical gestures such as shaking hands or hugging.

Conclusion

The reality of community life for adults with learning disabilities can be, as Bayley (1997b) and Brechin (1998) state, both superficial, and a 'struggle against stereotyped attitudes and expectations'. It is a more challenging, painful and dramatic version of that which we all experience: inclusion, exclusion, achievements and impossibilities. Music therapy groups offer a protected therapeutic space where together clients can explore the issues and challenges that arise as a result of greater involvement in their local communities. The groups described in this chapter provided a containing function where fantasies and projections, fears and joys could be expressed, shared and thought about in music and talk. The issues of independence, decision making, relationships, employment and disability were all brought into the group. Music therapy has a key role to play in assisting the transitions between different types of cultures and communities, and in enabling people to find their own ways of interacting and acting in their chosen communities.

Chapter 8

Working with people with profound and multiple learning disabilities in music therapy

Tessa Watson

> A new friend visiting us told us that Kathy was the first person with severe learning disabilities she had ever met. Within a very short time they were communicating very effectively . . . Was she especially sensitive, or did she just make the effort? She went on to do music therapy with people with multiple and learning disabilities, outstanding in her ability to communicate successfully with people no one else expected to respond.
>
> (Fitton 1994: 16)

This quotation, particularly appropriate to this book, introduces key themes about being with people with profound and multiple learning disabilities that will be explored in this chapter: the amount of effort that both communication partners must make, the expectation that there might not be a response, the sensitivity required to make a relationship, and the valuing of the work. The chapter focuses on the work that music therapists undertake with people with profound and multiple learning disabilities, with a consideration of their particular needs, a case study of a music therapy group, and guidelines for good practice.

Profound and multiple learning disabilities

People with profound and multiple learning disabilities have an estimated IQ of below 20, and additional disabilities (sometimes termed additional or complex needs). Lacey and Ouvry state that 'often the multiplicity of disabilities include sensory or physical impairment but others may be involved, such as autism or mental illness. Behaviour which may be very challenging and or self injurious may also be present' (1988: ix). Samuel and Pritchard list the characteristics of this client group as follows:

- extremely delayed intellectual and social functioning
- little or no apparent understanding of verbal language

- physical and sensory disabilities
- associated medical conditions
- need for constant support and supervision (2001: 39).

People with these disabilities may have varying specific diagnoses, but all will rely on others to meet their needs, and will have significant barriers to communication. There has been an increase in the population of adults with profound disabilities, due to greater longevity and higher survival rates of babies and young children with severe disabilities. This may mean a significant period of early life spent in hospital, and medical conditions in later life requiring treatment. Frequent health problems are eating, swallowing and weight problems, respiratory infections, epilepsy, and risk of pressure sores. With the transition to adulthood these health problems may increase, leading to more rather than less dependence on carers. As Sheehy and Nind note, mental health problems may be present though hard to diagnose: 'There is a range of evidence that suggests that there are likely to be significant, if as yet unmeasured, challenges to the mental health of people with profound and multiple learning disabilities' (2005: 35). These authors suggest that mental well-being can be supported 'through active personal and environmental interactions' (2005: 35), such as might be achieved in music therapy.

In 1992 Sinason wrote that 'the profoundly multiply handicapped individual can exist in a double vacuum where his or her own sense of bereavement and isolation is matched by the outside world's indifference, fear or hostility' (1992: 208). Ten years on, the UK Profound and Multiple Learning Disabilities (PMLD) Network echoes Sinason's words, stating that the specific needs of this group are not considered. They note that adults with profound and multiple learning disabilities are some of the most excluded and little valued people in our society, and that they and their families and carers need specific support (PMLD Network 2003).

Communication

It is important to respect and value people as they are in order to communicate in a way that is appropriate for them.

(Thurman *et al.* 2003: 84)

People with profound and multiple learning disabilities are usually unable to communicate in formal ways (such as speech, or a sign language such as Makaton). They might use eye contact, body language, facial expression or vocal sounds to communicate their preferences and express their feelings and experiences. Porter *et al.* (2001) note that the feelings and meanings behind these communications can be hard to interpret and verify. This can mean isolation from everyday experiences and contact with others. It may take a long period of time for a person with profound disabilities and a communication partner to find a way of being together and working together. McIntosh and Whittaker confirm the importance of finding meaningful ways to communicate when they state that 'communication is the precursor to social activity. It underpins confidence, equality, empowerment and friendship' (1998: 17). Working with clients to enhance their communication skills can develop self-advocacy, confidence and choice making.

Fitton, writing about her daughter Kathy, makes clear the difference between a description of Kathy's medical history and a description of her personality and likes and dislikes (1994: 6). Her book advocates for the need to find ways of communicating with people with profound disabilities in order that they can be known as people first. This idea is familiar to music therapists, whose approach enables a non-verbal, person-centred communication.

Living a full life

With the emphasis on people with learning disabilities taking a full part in their communities, day centres are becoming more community based. Clients with profound disabilities are likely to continue to need access to clinic or day centre based specialist health interventions such as arts therapies, occupational therapy, physiotherapy, and speech and language therapy input, and may find it particularly hard to integrate more fully into their communities. Specialist therapies such as music therapy provide an accessible therapeutic intervention which develops self-awareness and reciprocal relationships with others, aiding integration into everyday or community situations.

Working together

Person-centred planning and circles of support involve a committed group of people (including family) who meet with the client to think about their needs and wishes. This is particularly important for people with profound disabilities as it allows family or carers, friends and staff working with the client to communicate and share their knowledge and experiences of the client. Music therapists are often included in these planning forums.

In addition to formal meetings, families and carers may be given information so that they are aware of the nature of the therapy the client is being offered. Information sheets and reports about the process of the therapy are often shared with those involved with the care of the client. In a graphic example of a lack of communication about services that were offered to her daughter, Fitton writes that she didn't know how her daughter Kathy got on at respite care: 'She could not tell me, and no one else did' (1994: 106).

Whilst issues of confidentiality should be carefully considered when liaising with carers and colleagues, the sharing of insights gained in sessions can develop the holistic care offered to the client.

Supporting staff

Due to the demanding nature of the work, the turnover of staff working with clients with profound and multiple learning disabilities can be very high. One role for the music therapist can be to contribute towards support and development of staff through training. It is useful to meet with new staff during their induction period to give information about music therapy in order that they can support clients appropriately. Therapists might consider running workshops for groups of new staff, and may also offer supervision of music-based groups on an ongoing basis. In addition, care staff may also work in sessions with music therapists, which can help to develop experience, skills and a greater understanding of clients.

Music therapy strategies for working with people with profound and multiple learning disabilities

When working with clients who have profound disabilities, music therapists will consider each person's learning and physical disabilities in order to assess their individual needs in the music therapy setting. Physical disabilities may have an impact on how the client can use the instruments. It is helpful to be able to have a joint session with a physiotherapist in order to gain knowledge about specific movements and positioning that might assist the client to use the instruments fully. To this end, adapted instruments or beaters can be useful to include in the therapy room. Wigram reminds us:

> Before trying to explore what a person does in a music therapy session, and what they are bringing in their music to a relationship or an interaction, it is important to look at what they are physically or perceptually able to do. Poor control of movement, deficiencies in hand/eye co-ordination and an inability to focus on objects or instruments out of a limited visual range, are going to seriously limit the creative abilities of a person. This is particularly noticeable with physically or sensorily handicapped people, and the physical disability acts as a constraint on personality development.
>
> (Wigram 1988: 44)

Clients with profound disabilities may need a longer assessment period (for example eight to ten weeks) in order to familiarize themselves with the new situation and to access instruments. In addition, shorter sessions may be more manageable at first. To introduce the client to the therapist and the instruments, it can be useful to meet initially in the client's environment, perhaps taking an instrument as an object of reference. Sessions can be moved into the music therapy room when the client is more familiar with the therapist. It can be useful to offer a 10- or 15-minute session twice a week rather than one 30-minute session.

The therapist's musical approach may need to be adapted in order to work meaningfully with clients who have profound disabilities and barriers to communication, and who are likely to play little music. This issue will be discussed in the case study in this chapter. When thinking about the meaning and feelings of the music and happenings in the session, therapists need to remain aware that these cannot be confirmed with the client as might happen with clients with more verbal facility. The experience of the music therapist is therefore extremely important. Some of the client's feelings or opinions will remain unknown, though they will give important indications of their experience through non-verbal communication. Dialogue with carers and other professionals can add to a more rounded picture of the experience of therapy.

Theory as framework for clinical work

Writers such as Stern (1985) provide theories that can help music therapists to think about meaningful contact with clients with profound disabilities. Stern developed his concept of affect attunement in response to the question: 'How can you "get inside of" other people's subjective experience and then let them know that you have arrived there without using words?' (1985: 138). Stern's work was with mothers and infants, and whilst it is important not to make too literal a parallel with music therapy work, the idea of communication taking place through different modalities or channels has particular relevance to work with clients who may use as their language of communication body language, movement and facial expression as well as sound. Stern considered that the properties of emotional affect can be communicated by six types of behaviour, and describes this process as more sophisticated than imitation, giving the indication of a capacity for psychic intimacy, and allowing qualities of feeling or vitality affects to be shared (Stern 1985; see also Sobey and Woodcock 1999; Watson 1998, 2002). Intensive interaction, developed by Hewett and Nind (1994, 1998; see also Leaning and Watson (2006)) is also concerned with sharing qualities of feeling with children and adults with profound learning disabilities. Also developed from mother–infant research, intensive interaction gives workers a way of being with clients described as hard to reach or who have severe barriers to communication. The technique uses playfulness, spontaneity and sensitivity in interactions, to make and develop relationships with clients. The literature on intensive interaction is growing and is a useful resource for the music therapist coming to work with clients with profound disabilities.

Bion's ideas of containment and reverie allow us to consider ways in which we might work with clients with profound disabilities to receive feelings that the client may not yet be able to manage themselves, and feed them back in manageable form (Bion 1962a). Much of Winnicott's writing is also relevant to the work. His writing about play and creativity is inspiring for music therapists, who are bringing a creative and explorative play to the client with their music. Winnicott stated that 'it is in playing and only in playing that the individual child or adult is able to be creative and to use the whole personality, and it is only in being creative that the individual discovers the self' (1971: 54). Winnicott's ideas of holding, transitional phenomena, and the true and false self are all useful theories to hold in mind when working with people with profound disabilities.

Case study

The following case study describes group work that took place with four clients with profound and multiple learning disabilities over eight months for one hour a week in an adult learning disability day centre. Two music therapists worked with the group, and the case study will describe the process of the group and the experience of the therapists.

The group

Phillipa is a woman with profound and multiple learning disabilities of 38 years. She lives at home with her family. She has no formal means of communication, and uses sounds and facial expression to indicate her needs and wishes. It is thought that Phillipa's understanding is good. She uses a wheelchair and has very little controlled physical movement, and has fairly frequent hospital admissions due to respiratory infections. Phillipa has a strong personality and is eager to communicate with others, and despite severe disabilities contributed a lot of music to the group (vocal and instrumental).

Mohammed is a man with profound and multiple learning disabilities and significant physical disabilities. He is 38 years old and lives at home with his family. Mohammed is described as being 'cut off' from the world and hard to reach. He has no formal communication and it is hard to know how much he might understand. He uses a wheelchair and engages in self-stimulatory behaviours such as teeth grinding.

Jerry is a man with profound and multiple learning disabilities of 26 years. He appears quite reserved and finds it hard to communicate directly with others. It is thought that his understanding is quite good, though he does not use formal communication systems. Jerry lives at home with his family, and uses a wheelchair (he has good use of his arms and hands).

Betty is a woman with profound and multiple learning disabilities of 27 years, who also has a probable diagnosis of autism. She lives in a group home with four others. She is described as being cut off from her environment and finds it hard to find ways to communicate with others. She often wanders or sleeps at the day centre.

Setting up a group

When setting up the group, the therapists talked to care staff who had made referrals, as well as meeting and observing potential clients. Parents and carers were consulted as well as staff, and were informed about the nature and aims of the group, its length, the staff involved, and who to contact with queries.

Particular considerations relating to the therapeutic environment were taken into account. The choice of room was significant. Given that there was likely to be frequent silence, or soft, intermittent music, interruptions from sounds outside may have disrupted the session. We considered the physical abilities of the clients and the ways they were most comfortable and free to move, and decided to run a floor-based group in a therapy room away from the main day centre area. We placed mats around the edges of the room, a low table in the middle, and instruments on the table and the floor around the room. At the beginning of each group, non-ambulant clients were assisted to move from their wheelchairs on to beanbags or mats. This took time at the beginning and end, but ensured that the environment was accessible to the group. The therapists were also floor based for the majority of the session. Clients were able to reach for instruments and we were all at the same eye level, engendering a sense of equality. Instruments were carefully chosen for their sound qualities and accessibility. We bought additional small percussion instruments that could be sounded with little effort, used adapted beaters when appropriate, and used boom stands and careful placing to assist clients in their playing. Instruments were played with feet and body movement as well as hands. This physical environment was monitored and adapted as the group progressed.

Aims for the group

The broad aims for the group were to engage clients in a spontaneous, creative and expressive communication dialogue through the musical environment. More specific aims were as follows:

- to encourage communication through use of the musical medium
- to provide an environment where fluency in communication is experienced through the musical medium

- to provide opportunities for group members to share and express aspects of their personalities and feelings
- to encourage interaction between group members and therapists
- to provide opportunities for group members to make choices
- to provide opportunities for group members to initiate and lead interactions
- to provide opportunities for group members to have control over events in the group
- to encourage liveliness and energy in musical interactions.

As we got to know the group, we added individual aims for each person. This helped the therapists to be clear about the purpose and direction of the group for each member.

The structure of the group

We planned a structure for the group which was reviewed on an ongoing basis. Whilst clients were supported to move from their wheelchairs, a pre-recorded tape was played to provide a neutral, open atmosphere. This tape was also played at the end of the group as clients were supported to leave the room, thus providing a musical landmark at the beginning and end of sessions.

The group then commenced with a hello song, especially composed for the group. One therapist sang with guitar accompaniment, the other therapist providing harmony on the violin. This provided rich, harmonic music to start the group. The therapists sang and played a chorus of the song to each person and then improvised with that person's mood, actions or sounds, reflecting their presence in the room. The personalities of each group member were thus clearly heard in the room from the start of the group. The hello song not only provided each group member with individual attention, helping them to recognize the setting they were in and to focus on the music, but also encouraged an awareness of who else was in the group.

A small percussion instrument was then passed around the group. This was partly to introduce different sensory and aural experiences to group members, and partly to introduce the different instruments that were available to them. Each group member was supported to explore the sound and feel of the instruments. This part of the session also emphasized the group circle and an awareness of turn taking.

The majority of the session was spent in improvisation. Sometimes this would start immediately with music from one or more of the clients, sometimes it would grow from silence. Instruments were sometimes selected and offered to group members. The improvisation section of the group was usually 20 to 25 minutes long.

In addition to this structure, the therapists thought carefully about how to prepare for breaks in therapy. We developed a sensory 'snake' of cardboard, with circles of textured fabric that were removed as a break approached. This was also used to prepare for the end of the group.

The group process – our starting point

Within a couple of weeks the hello song seemed to be recognized as the start of the group, and it was greeted by vocalizations from some group members. During the group improvisation there was initially little music initiated by the group. We found ourselves drawn to individual group members; it was hard to hear the group as a whole. The structured activities in the group gave us opportunities to get to know each group member better, and we realized that clapping, teeth grinding, physical movements (such as finger tapping or leg slapping) and eye contact were all part of the group's repertoire. This material was developed musically within the improvisations.

An initial theme of the group was absence or rejection. This included absence from the group due to illness and sleeping in sessions. Sometimes this sleeping was due to tiredness or a seizure, sometimes it seemed more of a defence against the close contact being offered. In the first few weeks, when the group was new and perhaps overwhelming, this may have allowed group members to regulate their contact with the group. Contact with the instruments and therapists was also rejected at times. This may also have been a way in which clients regulated their contact with the instruments (which were new objects) and the therapists (who were new workers). The therapists discussed together when to encourage engagement and offer instruments, and when to wait for an indication of readiness to participate.

Intentionality

In our discussions following the sessions, we found ourselves talking about the clients' actions in the sessions as being intentional or not. We discussed whether happenings that we heard or saw as being coordinated between group members were deliberately so. For example, we noticed that Mohammed danced with Phillipa's vocal sounds, and that Betty's walk matched the group pulse. We treated these links as meaningful and communicative (as the mother does with the infant) in order to encourage intentional interaction (Grove et al. 2000; Bradshaw 2001).

We noticed that sounds associated with self-absorbed or self-soothing behaviour began to be directed outwards and become more intentionally communicative as they were responded to in music. When watching the video in later sessions, it appeared clear that these connections were often initiated with exquisite timing, in direct connection with fellow group members. Physical happenings in the group also became more intentional, with eye contact and gaze becoming more deliberate, and the two ambulant group members choosing where to sit.

The music

The therapists gave a lot of thought to their musical input, and the way in which it could help each group member to find their own music and liveliness. Often one of the therapists would use a long melodic containing line, while the other responded to contributions from individuals. It felt important to use our melodic instruments (violin and cello), to provide a rich, harmonic musical environment. We thought about the timbre and pitch of our playing and adjusted our musical input from week to week. Often, chromatic music seemed to bring the group to life, perhaps because it provided harmonies and sounds that could encompass some of the group members' unconventional material (shouting, grunting, teeth grinding and movement). Singing was also important, as it enabled an immediate connection with group members who were able to respond vocally. Graham writes about the importance of vocal work and of the therapist developing a repertoire of musical responses when working with these clients (2004).

During discussion the therapists became aware of a shared feeling that the improvisation was the central part of this group. However, we also experienced a temptation to keep the improvisation short because of thoughts that nothing might happen. It was sometimes hard to know how long to wait for material to emerge from the group. In some sessions it took a long while before group members were able to contribute sounds, but gradually they developed familiarity and confidence and began to contribute material more quickly and spontaneously. The improvisation was the part of the group which allowed each member to bring their individual personality, music and creativity. Initially the therapists provided the overarching shape for the group's music, using musical elements such as tonality, pulse or melody to provide structure and coherence. However, as the group progressed and the material provided from the clients increased, the therapists did not always need to provide such structure.

Percussion instruments were introduced by reflecting clients' sounds (for example, Betty's tapping of fingers on a drum), and then offering the instrument to the client for their use. The repertoire of preferred sounds developed as the group progressed. For example, we noted that Mohammed enjoyed tapping an instrument held on his lap, and offered him the guitar, in order that he could feel greater resonance. We placed instruments near Phillipa's feet where she could kick them to make a loud sound.

Resistance and defensiveness

Resistance and defensiveness continued to be themes for the group. Some group members continued to use defences in order to moderate contact. For example, Betty would apparently fall asleep when the therapists' attention was directed towards her (during the hello song), but on watching the video was observed to wake up when this attention had passed. Sometimes Jerry did not want to get out of his chair at the beginning of the group and deliberately discarded beaters or instruments that had been placed for his use, and Mohammed ground his teeth as though keeping himself in his self-stimulatory world. We felt that there was interest in the therapists and instruments, but it was challenging for the group to engage actively. It took time for group members to feel able to use the instruments, and some clients did not play very often. Additionally, once clients became familiar with ways of playing or particular instruments, they could find it hard to try new things.

Graham writes about resistance to communication, stating that some clients 'appear to have developed no alternative means of communicating and seem determined to shut other people out as much as possible. Their evasive or defensive strategies might include shouting, rocking backwards and forwards and pushing away anyone who comes too close. An opportunity to make a choice could be responded to with anger' (2004: 25). The group offered an alternative means of communicating but also presented a challenge to the members.

Development of the group's music

As the group became established and we knew each other better, we became more aware of the different types of sounds and other material provided by the group members. We noticed Betty's vocal 'whooshing' sound and her perfectly timed sniffing – tiny contributions to the musical richness. We noticed how she kicked and sounded instruments as if by accident as she passed them. Mohammed began to touch instruments much more frequently, and Betty picked up instruments and began to throw them, creating dramatic sounds for the group. Nearly all of the clients developed the use of their voices, in their different ways. Phillipa's singing was soloistic and profoundly moving. She was totally at home, fully engaged in the process of the group and we wondered if this could be so in any other setting.

We developed our ability to accept varied and different material from the group, and to respond to tiny sounds as well as to movement and facial expression. In addition, we felt less pressured to play ourselves. We became more aware of silence and its place in the musical soundscape of the group. The attention and focus of the group developed, and we noticed more alert expressions. Silence no longer felt like a void but had more of an antici-patory quality.

We thought each week about where to place instruments so that they could be found and used (for example, so that Phillipa could kick a drum and Betty could find instruments to pick up, drop or throw). We were aware of the importance of timing. Offering an instrument at the right time could make a difference to whether the client would be able to accept it or not (akin to Winnicott's 1971 ideas about object presenting).

Use of the environment

As well as developments in music and interaction, there were changes in the ways in which the group members could use the environment. It seemed as though they felt more able to make an impact upon the physical space. Several group members developed their use of body language. For example, Mohammed made stronger movements with his arms and legs, and Betty often stood up, made a pose, and then sat down next to someone new (her choice of companion seemed carefully chosen). There was a growing sense that group members were making choices about whether to take an instru-ment, play, and where to sit. These quantitative changes were observed week by week and helped us as therapists to know that the group was changing and developing.

Changes and developments

Over the eight months of the group there were many changes. The group seemed to offer both a positive experience and a challenge to group members, who expressed joy, pleasure, frustration and anger during the process of the group. Some group members developed skills and abilities, such as intentional vocal communication, and handling and using instru-ments. Direct interactions were developed between both client and thera-pists and between clients. The therapists did not always need to initiate or support interactions, and this indicated greater independence and con-fidence in this group setting. Some clients began to bring more physical movement to the group and were able to use the instruments in a more physical and deliberate way. Despite their profound disabilities the clients were able to make music together, and at times individual clients were able to lead the music. Some of these changes were also noted in other environ-ments by other staff, and have been maintained over time.

The group became a place where clients appeared to experience profound moments of communication and connection. It was often a very energetic and exciting experience.

Working together

Each week the therapists spent time after the group discussing the work and planning for the next session. We aimed to discuss openly what we each felt was happening in the group. Detailed notes including plans for the next week were made, and we took time to consider our musical input, discussing the different ways that we had played and how we might develop this to work with the group.

Working together allowed us to discuss difficult issues, share thoughts and support each other. In the initial sessions of the group, we both experienced the challenge of providing meaningful music when we had little material from the group to work with. When one therapist was away and the other ran the group on her own, it felt hard to manage the practicalities of the group and provide a musically containing environment. Paradoxically, it seemed more essential to have two music therapists in this group, where there was little music, than in other groups where music was plentiful.

We reflected on the roles of the therapists and the ways in which these changed. Initially we felt responsibility to provide music for the group, and we thought about this and the feelings that arose when we sat in silence. We discussed what we thought *should* be happening and the expectations we needed to lay aside to allow the group to develop in its own way. We also shared the impact the group had for us: admiration, humour, frustration, anger and sadness were emotions that we experienced in the work. Sinason's quotation is apposite here:

> Although we are all disabled in different ways there is a major qualitative difference in the psychic experience of severe learning disability. To deny the emotional experience of this difference is to handicap any possible treatment. This means coming to terms with the guilt of not being learning disabled.
>
> (1999: 446)

After the ending

Following the group, reports were written and the therapists met with key workers and fellow professionals to discuss the work that had taken place, and any recommendations. Some recommendations related to activities that could be developed by care staff (e.g. intensive interaction, musical and sensory activities). Others related to the timing or process of engaging a client, or the environment which seemed to help participation to occur. Another group was run a year later and carers were encouraged to re-refer clients where this was felt appropriate.

Acknowledgements

With thanks to those who gave permission for therapy work to be described in the case study. Names and details have been changed in order to maintain privacy. With thanks and acknowledgements to Minna Harman, music therapist.

Chapter 9

Looking in from the outside

Communicating effectively about music therapy work

Ben Saul

Introduction

In a thoughtful commentary on Britain's relationship with its disabled population, Ian Dury typifies a British tradition of satire in his song 'Spasticus Autisticus' (1981). He criticizes a society celebrating the year of the disabled child whilst ignoring the actuality of many disabled people, reflexively ostracized by their local communities and denied any meaningful control over their own lives. Twenty-four years on, the sculpture of Alison Lapper, naked, pregnant and disabled, presides over the northwest corner of Trafalgar Square sparking a fresh debate on society's relationship with disability. People with learning disabilities are still having to demand recognition as people who are able to communicate their strength, survival and a 'relentless need to be taken seriously' (Ritchie 1993a: 91) where those around them allow it.

Those around them are encouraged to develop a person-centred approach to planning services as a 'mechanism for reflecting the needs and preferences of a person with a learning disability . . . based on social inclusion, civil rights, choice and independence' (DOH 2001c: 49). It is expected that all professionals, including music therapists will engage in person-centred planning with 'people with profound and complex disabilities [who] may have difficulty communicating their needs and wishes' (p. 101). This individual planning can be achieved through the delivery of a continuously improving, evidence-based and quality service run by skilled, trained and qualified staff working in partnership with all other relevant services (p. 26).

What are the possible implications for music therapists engaging in this way of working? One implication is likely to be that allied professionals and carers working with this client group may begin to ask the following questions of music therapists:

- Does music therapy intervention support social inclusion?
- Does music therapy develop a service user's ability to be in control of their life and make life choices?

- Is there evidence of music therapy services having a significant role in improving health for these people?
- Does involvement with music therapy positively affect staff performance in learning disability services?

Can music therapists engage in a debate around these questions with their fellow professionals and find opportunities to develop the services they offer? Historically, music therapy practice developed in response to the introduction of new philosophies of care. As Bunt recalls, initially the experience of music therapy 'could do nothing but good' for any client group. Gradually 'more systematic reasons for referral were itemized' (1994: 9). Music therapy has to keep reviewing its identity in order to 'indicate its efficacy and hold its own in the open market place' (p. 160).

Recent research conducted by this author examined the provision of music therapy for service users of an organization working with adults with learning disabilities in South East London (Saul 2004). Staff were asked to complete a questionnaire to answer the following questions:

- Is music therapy an effective and valuable clinical intervention for people with severe learning disabilities and challenging behaviour?
- Do service users benefit from the music therapist's multidisciplinary approach to working?
- Could other professionals understand their clients better through understanding the benefits of their music therapy input?
- Would service users gain a clear extra benefit from this association?

For those looking in from the outside in this organization, an understanding of what clients were engaged in and achieving in music therapy could only come about if the music therapist was able to communicate effectively about what was taking place. The ability to communicate with other key workers has been recognized as an important aspect of the work of music therapists for many years (Moss 1999; Ritchie 1993a; Toolan and Coleman 1995). Where person-centred approaches are being adopted, communicating effectively about music therapy work becomes an intrinsic part of the clinical process. If clients are better understood because staff awareness and understanding is enhanced through music therapy input, the efficacy of music therapy can be judged in a new, evidence-based way.

The questionnaire

Professionals and carers involved with the music therapy service completed a questionnaire, which aimed to find out how they thought music therapy had affected the lives of the service users they worked with. Those who took part in interviews included front line care staff, management staff, members of the local primary care trust and allied health professionals, including speech and language therapists. This represented all staff who had been involved with music therapy, meaning that a complete population study was conducted (Oppenheim 1992: 44). Staff were invited to progressively focus on aspects of the lives of service users and the value of music therapy intervention for them. They were also encouraged to talk freely about their hopes for service users experiencing music therapy. The following themes were explored in the questionnaire and interviews.

Control and communication

Staff were asked for their perceptions of the ability of service users to actively plan and be in control of their lives, and how they felt music therapy could support this. Respondents mostly felt that service users needed to experience increased levels of control through being better supported by staff and improving their communication skills. The need for clients to develop confidence was a common theme in responses. One member of staff considered that their clients being more in control of their lives meant having a greater ability to influence the dynamics of the relationships they were in and, for example, gain 'ownership of a role in their family'.

It was considered that music therapy gave service users an experience of being in control in a therapeutic relationship, allowed them to 'develop communication' and 'find new ways of expression'. A number of staff felt that developing relationships in a safe and non-judgemental environment encouraged service users to become more confident in their relationships in the wider world. One person suggested that as a relationship developed in music therapy, service users were being helped to 'take a fully active part in [their] life'.

This comment resonates particularly with Ritchie's work, referred to in the introduction to this chapter, where she shows that people with severe learning disabilities and challenging behaviour can be worked with in the music therapy relationship by looking at challenging behaviour as not just negative and destructive but as a communication of strength, survival and a 'relentless need to be taken seriously' (1993a: 91). Where the music therapist interprets the actions of service users, either musically or verbally, as part of the music therapy process, a relationship is built between therapist and client that supports change from institutionalized lifestyles, enabling service users to become 'more spontaneous and free thinking people' (p. 101).

Sharing knowledge about social communication

Whilst music therapists have a responsibility to communicate directly with those outside the session about the work in music therapy, we might ask if they can also make communication between client and carer easier? Kevan argues that challenging behaviour occurs when there is a mismatch between the poor receptive language abilities of the person with learning disabilities and the expressive communication of others. Kevan observes that 'it is reasonable to suggest that the partner without communication disability is better placed than the adult with a learning disability to learn and implement new communication strategies' (2003: 76). Kevan suggests a useful shift of research focus that could take place. Examining the roles of people who care for service users may help to understand the roots of behaviours described by Bell and Espie as those that 'challenge services' (2002: 19). If staff are responsible for establishing what Kevan refers to as the communication environment, 'the extent to which the communication environment matches the receptive abilities of the individual may have an impact on the frequency of behaviours that lead to access to, or escape from the experience of communication for the individual' (2003: 76).

Enabling more productive communication between client and carer is not a simple task, but one that could improve the communication skills and confidence of individuals, leading to an increase in 'the range and frequency of their behaviours rather than increasing or decreasing selective aspects of their repertoire of behaviours and abilities' (Macleod *et al.* 2002: 36).

The reality for people with severe learning disabilities and challenging behaviour is that greater social inclusion and control in their lives cannot happen without the development of some personal abilities that enable them to be properly equipped to access their community. For many of these service users there is a primary need to learn and develop basic interpersonal skills. In order for this to happen professionals working with this group also need to develop their own interpersonal skills and abilities, much in the way described by Kevan, to directly meet service users 'level of receptive communication skill (capacity to understand)' (2003: 79). Music therapists clearly have the necessary abilities to develop a significant role in the training and supervising of staff seeking these skills, as suggested by Graham (2004), Sinason (1992) and described by Toolan and Coleman (1995: 20).

Social functioning

Through the questionnaire, staff perceptions of service users' social needs and potential were gained, as well as the ways in which they felt music therapy could provide a tool to develop social functioning. Workers felt strongly that service users needed to improve their social presence, be more active and have a more positive social experience in their lives. They considered that this could be achieved in a number of ways, dependent on the abilities of individual service users. Thus, improvements in social functioning ranged from service users spending more time with each other, to others being encouraged to take opportunities in the community through the increased use of public transport.

It was reported that music therapy could support improved access to the community, and increased community activity. The nature of the music therapy session, aimed at responsively involving participants, was seen to stimulate activity, a sense of self, responsiveness to others and a platform for social exploration, within and outside of the sessions. As one respondent commented, music therapy 'helps them to be more valuable and participate in their community'.

Whether the traditional boundaries of an individual's community consisted of their home, the day centre and the bus that took them in between, or the whole of South East London, music therapy helped staff to think about ways that boundaries could be extended or social experience could be enriched. One respondent, thinking about two particular clients she worked with, was enthused about the staff- and client-led music that now took place at the community home they shared following music therapy. With regular soirées around the karaoke machine, music underpinned the everyday experience in the house and housemates could be 'involved in their own entertainment and celebrations'. However, music therapists cannot solely focus on the social needs of people with severe learning disabilities and challenging behaviour. Those with the most complicated emotional problems cannot easily be accommodated in sessions if music therapy is set up solely as a social activity session (Hooper 2002: 167), and involvement in music cannot easily be shown to improve social skills (Duffy and Fuller 2000: 87).

Sharing knowledge about social potential

Graham's work with learning disabled adults preparing for 'integration in the community' (2004: 24) shows how the music therapist can also engage with the emotional world of people she describes as 'pre-verbal and non-verbal' in order to develop community presence. Framing this work in theories of interaction and communication in child development, Graham considers the challenges that face care staff in responding appropriately to the difficulties or barriers to communication.

One of her conclusions is that music therapists may be usefully employed helping staff to become more aware of 'the various nonverbal ways of communicating employed by their service users' (2004: 27). Graham acknowledges that it is more difficult to maintain multidisciplinary links working in community settings, and she states that for community staff 'it is more important than ever for therapists, consultants, key workers, and other staff to maintain links with each other and to ensure that they are pooling their skills and resources instead of working in isolation' (p. 27).

Where emotional connections between the music therapist and service user are seen by staff (such as those defined by Watson 1998: 90) it is easier to explore service users' social needs, both in sessions and when planning further interventions with staff. Music therapists can usefully involve care staff in the thought processes and clinical experiences that shape their work. Sinason raises the concern that 'the profoundly multiply handicapped individual can exist in a double vacuum where his or her own sense of bereavement and isolation is matched by the outside world's indifference, fear or hostility' (1992: 208). In the case of the organization taking part in this research project, Sinason's outside world is populated both by those who completed questionnaires, and local communities in a broader sense. If the music therapy process can allow therapist and client to safely explore the emotional world, the music therapist is well placed to communicate with those outside about the conditions a learning disabled person is living in. When staff considered the efficacy of music therapy in providing better health, the impact of the intervention on emotional functioning was considered significant.

Better health

Staff commented on the way they felt music therapy could help service users lead healthier lives. They felt that the development of emotional expression and emotional self-management would help service users to lead a more healthy life, and music therapy was felt to support healthy living because it supported physical, social and emotional development. In particular, those that had attendant difficulties, such as sensory impairment or physical disabilities, were felt to be having their health needs met in music therapy.

Ross and Oliver assess aspects of emotional functioning of adults with severe and profound learning disabilities from a health perspective using a psychometric measure for depression and quality of life. They acknowledge that 'indirect methods are the only means available for investigating mood and emotions in individuals with severe learning disabilities or no expressive language' (2003: 89). Music therapy, particularly as presented in Toolan and Coleman (1995), Watson (2002) and Saul (2004) could be promoted as a method for investigating mood and emotions and engaging depressed clients, particularly those with no expressive language.

Sharing knowledge about music therapy

Music therapy must be commissioned as a 'specialized treatment that offers clients a way to address problems in their lives' (Watson 2002: 102). It needs to be consistently presented to other professionals as primarily a health service and not the music activity session or lesson most expect. By the end of this project, music therapy was consistently referred to as a therapy and the client's experience was referred to in terms of development where clients were felt to progress in aspects of their functioning.

People with learning disabilities must be provided with a health service that is designed around their individual needs. If music therapy is perceived as being able to improve the emotional language skills of service users and effect change in the lives of service users outside music therapy sessions, it can be regarded as an extremely versatile health intervention based on core values of engagement with service users at an emotional level.

Partnership working

Responses to the questionnaire showed that staff felt partnership working was a valuable tool that can be utilized to provide a better service for their clients. Some respondents felt that the experience of not only clients but also staff in music therapy led to more effective working relationships being established between staff and clients. One staff member commented on the clear communication from the therapist about how others were expected to behave in and around music therapy sessions. This was felt to lead to a consistency being developed around the experience of music therapy for client, staff and music therapist.

Communicating effectively

The lack of an appropriate and considered response to the communicated needs of people with learning disabilities potentially denies them their right to have basic social and emotional needs met, even when professionals might feel they are doing a good job:

> Cleaning people's mess continuously, as a way of not managing to stay with their emotional experience is only the flip side of shouting at them aggressively. Being close to something that has gone wrong is a permanent reminder of the frailty of the human body and mind. Where staff are not helped to deal with that there is no possibility of an attempt to link the incontinence to any emotional disturbance or to anger or depression. There is no attempt to think of a behavioural programme or provide such facilities as art or music or drama therapy.
>
> (Sinason 1992: 208)

Arthur (1999) and Brown and Smith (1992) argue for the provision of psychological consultation to staff responsible for the care and support of people with learning disabilities. Arthur (2003) argues that such support 'facilitates [service users'] emotional development, improves staff–client relationships, decreases symptomatic behaviour and helps improve quality of life' (2003: 28).

Bell and Espie (2002), looking at the complex emotional relationships front line care staff have with both service users and their management (the social context where challenging behaviour mostly exists), suggest that it is critical to ensure all such relationships remain positive and supportive so that a healthy social environment can be maintained for service users. They recommend that studies might be commissioned that examine individual staff members' feelings towards service users in relation to how effectively they feel they cope with service users.

Saul's study (2004) shows that through experience of music therapy sessions, a wide range of professionals felt they could develop a better understanding of the benefits of music therapy for service users and also service users' broader relationship with their environment. This implies that music therapy can be used as a partnership working resource that can develop more 'appropriately skilled, trained and qualified' professionals and develop 'a better understanding of the needs of people with learning disabilities amongst the wider work force' (DOH 2001c: 26).

Conclusion

Does music therapy intervention support social inclusion? Does music therapy develop a service user's ability to be in control of their life and make life choices? Is there evidence of music therapy services having a significant role in improving health for these people? Does involvement with music therapy positively affect staff performance in learning disability services?

Developing the emotional expression and emotional self-management skills of both clients and staff allows music therapists to show that they can offer a service that is beneficial to people with learning difficulties, and can therefore answer these questions positively.

Clearly, developing increased community presence for people with severe learning disabilities and challenging behaviour is the best way that society at large can be encouraged to reassess how welcoming local communities are for people with disabilities. Developing more opportunities for service users to be in control of their lives and involved with planning their future allows people with learning disabilities to realize that professionals are working with their best interests at heart. Meaningful relationships can be established over time between service users and sensitive professionals throughout their lives, and person-centred approaches help to facilitate this. Person-centred approaches need to be developed in conjunction with clinical interventions such as music therapy, that aim to increase both the communicative potential of people with disability and the communication abilities of the professionals working with them.

Bunt (1994) described the need for music therapists to develop 'solid outcome work, indicating changes related to objectives across many parameters' that would lead to areas of research involving deeper levels of analysis (p. 164). Staff responding to this study gave a clear indication that music therapy could support their clients in gaining greater access to their wider communities and experiencing more opportunity and control in planning their lives.

Acknowledgements

Ben Saul would like to thank the following for their encouragement and support: Greenwich NHS Teaching Primary Care Trust, tutors at Roehampton University, the Research Support Unit, staff at Three C's Lewisham and Adrian Crockford.

Chapter 10

Multidisciplinary working and collaborative working in music therapy

Karen Twyford and Tessa Watson

Introduction and literature review

> Professionals will join a team only if they perceive it to be in their interest to co-operate or at least in the client's interest for some kind of co-ordination.
>
> (Ovretveit 1993: 5)

With this quotation in mind, it is interesting to consider that many music therapists think it important to be employed as part of a multidisciplinary team. Hills *et al.* (2000) established this in their study, showing it is possible that music therapists can gain satisfaction from working with colleagues from different backgrounds and that a greater sense of personal accomplishment can be provided by working as part of a multidisciplinary team. Eisler confirms this further when she writes that music therapists can 'draw sustenance and support from the combined or individual wisdom of the members of the team, with opportunities for growth and a shared understanding of common problems' (1993: 23). Although there will inevitably be sources of pressure in teamworking, Hills *et al.* (2000) identify that working in a team, feeling appreciated by others and gaining support from colleagues are significant rewards for the music therapist. All of this indicates that considerable personal benefit can be gained from being employed in a multidisciplinary team. These themes will be expanded in the multidisciplinary discussion in this chapter.

In comparison to other professions music therapy is relatively new to multidisciplinary working. This has meant that music therapists have had to work hard to defend and validate their work and position within the team and this dedication has been positive for the profession as advocated by Eisler (1993). In striving for recognition music therapists have achieved accreditation alongside a multiplicity of professions registered with the Health Professions Council. However, music therapists still feel that they have to gain acceptance to be a part of the multidisciplinary team and this can only be achieved when music therapy is valued, understood and proven effective (Eisler 1993; Odell-Miller 1993). An important question is how it is possible to achieve this, for as Jacobs (2000) concludes in her study, music therapy is not often fully understood by other members of the multi-disciplinary team and potential referrers to music therapy. Odell-Miller and Darnley-Smith (2001) believe that it is perhaps through co-working with other professions that the process of the work of music therapists is con-solidated. This suggests that collaborative working can encourage a greater understanding of the role of music therapy and should be considered by music therapists working in teams.

It is evident that the combined efforts of a multidisciplinary team can be of great benefit to the client, although this can be difficult to achieve at times (Watson et al. 2004). A greater understanding of clients can be achieved through the contribution of specialist knowledge from various professions, including insights from music therapy (Durham 2002; Ritchie 1993b). Additionally, the sharing of different perspectives and skills within the team will benefit the professionals involved (Watson 2002). Multi-disciplinary teamwork can offer the music therapist many possibilities for extending clinical work. However, it can raise significant issues for some music therapists. While it is important to demonstrate to the team the potential of music therapy and how it can work, the right balance of multidisciplinary teamwork is essential to ensure that client boundaries and confidentiality are not impinged upon (Odell-Miller 1993; Ritchie 1993b).

Considering these issues, we can see that music therapists undertake successful multidisciplinary teamwork at four levels. The most fundamental of these is the *communicative* level, where the music therapist liaises with other professionals to share important information regarding a client. At this level music therapy intervention is distinct from other services offered. However, many music therapists suggest that team members may share ideas and use a common language to discuss and compare therapeutic changes (Aldridge et al. 1990; Aldridge and Aldridge 1992; Smeijsters 1993).

At an *interactive* level music therapists work collaboratively with other team members towards shared aims and objectives and sometimes these may be in addition to their music therapy aims. They may also work in parallel with other therapists or professionals with sessions provided separately in each medium but planned to include similar themes (Zagelbaum and Rubino 1991; Goldstein-Roca and Crisafulli 1994).

Multidisciplinary teamworking at a *facilitative* or *observational* level occurs when team members from different professional backgrounds are present in sessions together, but one therapist leads the session. Therapists functioning at this level may find their roles change depending on which modality they are working in (Watson and Vickers 2002). While the client only experiences one medium at a time, the presence of a therapist or professional from a different discipline will be influential. Working at this level is also useful for observational reasons which may include the interpretation of responses or the education of others (for example, demonstrating the potential of music therapy with shared clients).

Music therapists working at a fully *integrated* level combine their approaches with other professionals and work simultaneously with different disciplines and professions to provide a unique combination of therapeutic intervention for the benefit of clients. There is a shared purpose which has the potential to provide a meta-perspective (Wilson and Pirrie 2000). The advantages of multidisciplinary teamwork at this level can be described as complementary, successful in stimulating fresh and creative approaches and for providing opportunities for communication and shared interaction to happen (Slivka and Magill 1986, cited in Decuir 1991; Finlay *et al.* 2001; Kennelly *et al.* 2001; Walsh Stewart 2002). Working at this level also provides the opportunity for music therapists to learn about other approaches and question, adapt or reinforce their own techniques (Walsh Stewart 2002).

We can see from these four different levels of multidisciplinary work that there are many reasons why music therapists employed in teams consider multidisciplinary working at different levels.

Benefits and challenges of multidisciplinary clinical work

It is probable that the majority of music therapists will work as part of a multidisciplinary team at some point in their career. They will discover that multidisciplinary working with other colleagues at a variety of levels is essential for effective practice and survival within the team. In this part of the chapter we consider both the benefits and the issues that challenge the music therapist and the profession of music therapy when employing multidisciplinary approaches within clinical work. The following ideas are formed from data collected for a research project undertaken in 2004 (Twyford 2004; Twyford and Watson in press).

Ultimately, multidisciplinary clinical work provides a holistic approach and benefits the client. The sharing of specialist knowledge from more than one discipline can provide a greater understanding of clients. If undertaken with clear planning and specific purpose, a multidisciplinary approach ensures the coordination of appropriate input, and can also provide continuity of care, which is imperative for client change and progress. In some instances, it is appropriate to use multidisciplinary work as an assessment of needs in preparation for ongoing therapy. In addition, the process of joint working draws attention to other aims of the multidisciplinary team and these may be incorporated into future music therapy work.

Multidisciplinary clinical work can be useful both in establishing a new music therapy service within a team, and in consolidating an existing music therapy service by assisting others to gain a greater understanding of the discipline and the way in which it relates to their own discipline through first-hand experience. Working in this way can promote openness among team members, assisting in the creation of clear communication channels, support for those in isolated positions and the resolution of issues of conflict with colleagues. A more cohesive and efficient service can ensue when colleagues from different professions are familiar with what others can offer. The experiential nature of multidisciplinary clinical work not only provides an insight into the work of others but also helps the music therapist to realize new perspectives for their own work, thereby promoting the development of professional skills. At a functional level multidisciplinary clinical work can provide the music therapist with a sense of identity and belonging which is imperative to teamworking.

However, multidisciplinary clinical work will inevitably raise issues relating to therapeutic boundaries and the identity of the music therapist and the profession of music therapy. It will require the music therapist to assume different roles within the collaborative partnership which may be challenging. The aim is therefore to create a fluid professional relationship so that the identities of the professionals involved are not obscured and professional boundaries are observed. This generates a sound understanding of each profession concerned and greater scope for reflection.

On a personal level multidisciplinary clinical work can be stimulating, refreshing, complementing and enriching for the music therapist. Working closely with other professionals can help music therapists to cope with the emotional impact of their work as a shared understanding amongst colleagues is generated. Ideas and approaches learnt from other professionals can be incorporated into music therapy practice by adapting techniques learned and using them in a musical way. The challenges that arise from multidisciplinary clinical work can be viewed as positive and can allow the individual to develop both professionally and personally as a music therapist. Although many music therapists employ these approaches and view them as crucial to their work and the development of the profession, issues of professional protectionism inhibit others from exploring the innovative potential of multidisciplinary clinical work and the possibilities it generates for the field of music therapy.

An ever-changing working culture indicates that it is necessary for music therapists to employ new and creative techniques and approaches in order to survive. The exposure that multidisciplinary clinical work provides is vital in realizing the potential of music therapy and this may lead to the creation of new positions, extended working hours in existing positions and an increase in referrals from other professions. However, one of the greatest benefits that multidisciplinary clinical work brings is to gain acceptance and raise the profile for the profession of music therapy. These ideas are now illustrated through the presentation of a multidisciplinary dialogue between team colleagues, who discuss their understanding of the nature of music therapy and the way in which the profession contributes to a team.

A multidisciplinary dialogue: the role of music therapy in a team

This dialogue, taken from a live discussion between five members of a community learning disability team, gives an insight into the ways in which health professionals from four disciplines view music therapy and work with the music therapist in the team. The professionals involved in the conversation are Alison (speech and language therapist), Manga (consultant psychiatrist), Sheila (community learning disability nurse), Brian (clinical psychologist) and Tessa (music therapist). They have had various degrees of contact with each other in the team, ranging from multidisciplinary discussion to collaboratively running groups.

Contact with music therapy

Sheila: I've certainly learnt a lot about music therapy since working in learning disabilities. I feel that it has a large part to play in learning disabilities as it's so important for people who are non-verbal. The main reason is to enable communication and express emotions.

Manga: I insisted we have a music therapist [in the team], because that was the first time that I was asked 'what therapists would you like to have?' and I said music therapist, definitely one of them. But I wasn't that sure that we would get one!

Sharing our different perceptions of what music therapy is

Sheila: I would say that the first thing a music therapist does is to develop a therapeutic relationship with that person, and enable them to express their inner, conscious and unconscious thoughts and feelings.

Alison: I could say something completely different – that it's about creating a space and an opportunity. You put together this group in this room, with the instruments, and then you facilitate the communication that can occur, and then in addition, there's all the emotional side of it.

Brian: I think it's about holding people's emotions, providing a place for them to release their feelings; then acknowledging them, accepting them and reflecting them back through music to validate their experience.

Manga: Sometimes you can't talk to patients to find out how they are feeling, so their inner world is accessed through art and music – they can express that very much. Even people who don't know about music, when they touch a musical instrument or come to music they can respond. I think that, especially for learning disabilities, it's an important area isn't it? Also, there are no side effects, there are no negative things about music therapy! Because of our disciplines and the way we think, we all look at it differently, don't we? For me it's about accessing the thoughts of the person's inner world, thinking about their mental state, and it's useful for me to know how they can express that (without being asked all these questions 'What are you thinking?' 'Are you hearing voices?' 'Is something bothering you?').

Alison: That's something that did strike me in the group [*Alison and Tessa have run a Music and Communication group together*], that people are completely unpressured, on the whole, whereas when we're doing our assessments, we need to prompt people so that we can see them at the top of their ability. In the music therapy setting you can play around with all sorts of aspects of the group in order to allow people to express themselves more, but it's completely left to the people to use that or not, there is so little pressure on people that it really helps them to use the situation.

How do you think music therapy is different from other disciplines?

Sheila: Well I can give a very clear example where I have a client with elective mutism, referred to psychology for therapeutic intervention but who wasn't able to use that approach because they didn't communicate verbally. And this client would have really benefited from music therapy – unfortunately there were other issues so she didn't attend, but there wouldn't have been any problems with her using music therapy.

Tessa: It's very non-threatening in that way, do you think?

Sheila: Definitely.

Alison: You haven't got to talk, and you haven't got to learn anything. You're not teaching people to play the instruments – when I was in the group, I was always wanting to try different things, but it's not always about that, is it?

Sheila: And maybe for a client the difficult intensity isn't there, say if you had to walk in, and you were face to face with a therapist, as opposed to having musical instruments which might be easier to use. Obviously, part of your role is to work with issues like low self-esteem, gaining eye contact, etc., but initially, somebody could come in and work in music therapy without making eye contact, etc. – whereas that's very difficult in a verbal or more traditional therapy.

Manga: Some highly autistic people who won't have any contact with people, they can interact with objects, which they can't do with people, so for them, it's good, it's the only kind of therapy one can offer, if nothing else can work. And for people with profound disabilities, it's such an achievement, if they make music it's their own creation. That's very important.

Brian: Yes, it's different because people are creating something very tangible, and it's being created with another person's accompaniment – and that's a different type of relationship than they might have with anyone else in their life.

Alison: In terms of differences, a lot of what the other disciplines are doing is quite verbally based isn't it? There's also a difference between what most of speech and language therapy does and what music therapy does in that on the whole our work is a lot more specific (for example, looking at a communication chart, or using signs and symbols), but what someone is getting from music therapy is the time and the space and the quality of interaction. And they can get used to that, the fact that it's going to go on for a certain amount of time. And certainly what we did in our group, although there were aims, the feeling was very much about here and now, and what's happening, and we'll see what happens.

Manga: It's much more psychotherapeutic, there's a free flow, free ventilation of issues.

Alison: And it's whatever the person decides to bring to it, because I feel we're often setting the agenda, we go in and do a particular piece of work, whereas in the music therapy group the feeling was not that at all, it's about here's a group of people and what do they want to happen, really, with some structure and thought about what they might need and how to structure the group.

What role does music therapy fulfil in a team?

Alison: As well as music therapy, in the training work that you're doing, like the intensive interaction training, you're helping other people to provide – not the same, but similar – opportunities, more frequently. So you're sharing skills, and hopefully service users are then given more opportunities where they can set the agenda, do what they want to do, lead an interaction etc. Which is great.

Tessa: So hopefully that quality of contact we were talking about gets spread a little.

Sheila: Also, you come to multidisciplinary team meetings, and share, not just the dynamics of the music therapy but also positive things about your relationship with the client, and contribute to the care plan on things like social issues, because you know that individual very well. You might know them better than anyone else, in fact it's very likely that you would. So it's not just music therapy, but . . .

Manga: – teamworking! [*All laugh.*]

Brian: I remember when you brought the team into your therapy room and we all sat and played music and made sound and you played back to reflect the team's music. I always thought that this was a profound experience and it brought the team together for those ten minutes. I wonder what potential there is for music therapy to help teams to be together, to connect and to reflect. I wonder if it was done on a regular basis whether some of the processes – conscious and unconscious – of the team could be considered?

What are effective ways of music therapists sharing information about what they do?

Manga: We have had really good workshops with you.

Tessa: That seems to be a good way to know about what happens in music therapy, because I can talk about it, but perhaps you need to experience it.

Manga: Oh yes, practical experience is definitely important.

Alison: Thinking about sharing knowledge and expertise, several joint groups have happened. You have worked with several of the speech and language therapists, and with the physiotherapist – I think that's such a worthwhile way of working. It's quite time intensive I guess but on the other hand it felt really worthwhile, bringing the two different ways of working together in a group.

Reflection on multidisciplinary discussion

This dialogue brings to life the ideas about music therapy and teamwork that were introduced at the beginning of the chapter. These colleagues talk about their belief that music therapy provides a non-pressured, nonverbal place for clients to build a relationship and develop their skills in the area of communication and interaction, as well as to work on specific emotional issues. They also state the value of working collaboratively with colleagues, and of providing knowledge and training (through music therapy and, in this case, intensive interaction workshops) in order that colleagues have an understanding of what clients will experience in music therapy, and to extend care workers' skills. The next part of the chapter considers what can happen in collaborative working between music therapists and other disciplines.

Collaborative working with other disciplines

Music therapists working in the area of adult learning disability engage in a significant amount of multidisciplinary and collaborative work. Hooper *et al.* state that 'as music therapists working with clients who have a developmental disability, we need to broaden our conception of music therapy and acknowledge the significant role that it can play when joined in therapeutic work with other modalities' (2004: 21). Within the remit of the NHS, many music therapists work in adult learning disability teams, with colleagues such as community nurses, occupational therapists, psychologists, physiotherapists, speech and language therapists, psychiatrists and care managers. Much of their work may be described as *communicative* or *interactive* (see p. 122). For example, a psychologist may work with a family providing advice about the management of difficulties, whilst a music therapist works individually with the client. A community learning disability nurse may provide input and support for specific health issues whilst a music therapist works with the client in a group setting on the resulting emotional and communication issues. Music therapists also work at a *facilitative* or *integrated* level with a variety of disciplines (including other arts therapists). The focus of this collaborative work will depend upon the needs of the clients, and the combined skills and goals of the collaborating professions. The roles of the therapists may be decided by the particular interests and experience of the workers, as well as their different areas of expertise. Thus there are many possibilities for combining expertise, clinical strategies and personal experience and approaches when working in this way. Two examples of collaborative clinical work are now given.

Art and music therapy group

This author has undertaken various collaborative projects with art therapy colleagues; some of this has been documented elsewhere (Watson and Vickers 2002). The work described here was undertaken in a group setting over approximately 25 sessions. The groups were constructed following referrals for clients around similar issues. Each group had a specific focus, such as managing anger, or loneliness and isolation. The first 12 therapy sessions were music therapy, followed by 12 of art therapy, with a visit to an art gallery in between to view images related to the theme of the group. The mediums of art and music were therefore used separately, rather than being combined. Other arts therapists have worked with the arts mediums used simultaneously. In the music therapy sessions, group music making was encouraged to share and express feelings related to the themes of the group. In the art therapy sessions, individual image making and occasionally group image making were used to enable clients to represent and explore their experiences.

Prior to the group the therapists discussed how they might run the sessions together, and decided upon an approach where the therapist whose art medium was being used would lead the session, with the other acting as co-therapist. This approach allowed each therapist to fully utilize their expertise in their particular medium. Whilst the therapists found that they had much in common in their training backgrounds and in the way that they might think about the work or run a session, it was useful to discuss theoretical and practical approaches and to find out more about the similarities and differences between the two professions. This process of discussion enabled both therapists to feel more confident working together, and also meant that they learnt more about the other profession.

Working together in this way provided clients with a rich therapeutic experience of two mediums, with the benefit of two therapists thinking together about the process of therapy. Additionally, it provided the therapists with a supportive and rewarding learning experience which deepened their understanding of the similarities and differences between the two disciplines, and of how each might help clients.

Music and communication group

This group was run jointly by a music therapist and speech and language therapist. It was set up to address issues of communication and interaction for clients with severe learning disabilities. The group ran for ten weeks and aimed to provide opportunities for clients to develop skills in the following areas:

- find different ways to greet, be with and say goodbye to each other
- interact freely with others
- gain attention and initiate contact
- make choices (say yes and no, choose instruments)
- share experiences with others and develop greater awareness of others
- express individual personalities and feelings.

These aims were met through the use of music, talk and Makaton sign language.

The therapists spent time considering their roles. In order that they felt confident about the smooth running of the group, a structured session plan was devised, including timings for each part of the session, which clearly detailed which therapist would run which part of the group. This was found to be very helpful at the beginning of the group process. As the group progressed, the therapists found themselves more confident in expanding their roles a little, and the speech and language therapist became more involved in the musical parts of the group, with the music therapist engaging more in the sections that involved Makaton and communication skills.

The common areas of expertise of the workers in this group were clearly in the areas of communication and interaction. Each worker valued the different skills of the other. For example, the music therapist valued a targeted approach to communication which provided a useful structure and focus for the group, and helped to measure progress for each person. The speech and language therapist found the non-directive and non-verbal approach of the music therapist allowed possibilities for communication and interaction to emerge naturally and with little pressure.

Guidelines for good multidisciplinary practice for music therapists

Successful collaborative multidisciplinary work results when the team gains an awareness of what music therapy is and how it can complement the roles of other team members, within a collaborative environment. An ability to work with others is essential, although the type of working will vary depending upon the culture and personalities in the team. In addition, professional and personal attributes are required of the music therapist.

The music therapist must be clear about their reasons for joint working and be aware that the presence of another professional in the therapeutic space will raise a diversity of issues. Initial discussion regarding the work is advantageous so that those involved are aware of what they hope to achieve from the collaboration. It is also advisable to inform managers so that their approval and cooperation is given. Prior to commencing collaborative work it is valuable to identify guidelines which consider the following elements:

1   The presence of other professionals will undoubtedly affect the dynamics of sessions (this may include bringing new styles of music). It may be useful to spend some time together before commencing clinical work, to allow professionals to familiarize themselves musically with each other.
2   The techniques and approaches of others may be markedly different from the music therapist's own and it is essential that these are discussed and treated with respect.
3   Likewise, other professionals' aims may be very specific and unrelated to the music therapist's aims. Both professionals' aims should be discussed prior to working together.
4   Inevitably the bridging of differing professional and theoretical worlds may be complex and will require the professionals involved to be able to make compromises.
5   The issue of boundaries and retaining of identities will need to be addressed and this can be achieved through continuous reflective dialogue by the professionals involved.

The music therapist should also be aware of the following professional and personal attributes that will be influential in creating a successful multidisciplinary partnership. These factors can be usefully discussed as the collaboration progresses:

1   Acknowledge that you can learn from others, particularly those in other professions.
2   Be open to working in different ways and incorporating different techniques into your practice.
3   Have confidence in your own skills.
4   Be prepared not to always lead, or always be right.
5   Be a good communicator.
6   Be accommodating of others as they discover and understand music therapy.

On an interpersonal level it is also important to be aware that the following personal qualities can encourage solid foundations for effective and productive collaborative practice:

• honesty
• flexibility
• supportiveness
• sensitivity
• acceptance
• understanding
• a sense of humour.

Finally, in order to ensure that a collaborative partnership succeeds, problems and issues should be discussed as they arise. This may take place following clinical sessions, or occasionally during sessions if this is appropriate. It may also be useful to set time limits on the collaborative work and review and extend these if necessary. The process of working collaboratively will be unique to the professionals undertaking it, who will develop both professionally and personally as they discover their own guidelines for working together.

Acknowledgements

With acknowledgements and thanks to Sheila Catton, Alison Germany, Brian Leaning and Dr Manga Sabaratnam for their involvement in this chapter.

Guidelines for good practice for music therapists

This Appendix gives suggestions for good practice for music therapists working with adults with learning disabilities.

Teamwork

- Good communication with both an immediate team and other partners is beneficial (e.g. organizations such as health, social services and Mencap). This communication can be developed through individual liaison regarding clients, and wider meeting and training forums.
- Workshops or training events offered to teams or partner organizations can enhance understanding of the role of the music therapist. This allows colleagues to support clients in therapy more effectively. Training sessions or induction meetings can routinely be offered to new staff at the point of induction.
- Music therapists can provide useful input to staff teams by offering supervision to staff running therapeutic or activity groups.

Communication

- When working with families consider the most appropriate way to make and maintain contact, and ensure that adequate and appropriate information is provided.
- Issues of ethnicity and culture are of importance; further information and assistance (e.g. translators) can be sought if required.
- Links with referring teams can ensure continuity of care at periods of transition.
- Links with music or arts therapists at local schools can ensure continuity of care at the time of school leaving. This may include meetings with school or paediatric therapists at strategic points in the year.
- Some areas have a protocol for contact with mental health services. Awareness of this and familiarity with the music or arts therapies departments in the locality can be useful.

Therapeutic administration

- It is useful to have a protocol for the process of therapy (including referral, assessment, treatment and discharge). Therapists might consider documenting this as a formal policy, in order to provide colleagues with a clear idea of how the service will operate. This also allows work to be audited against set standards. The use of accessible information (such as Makaton or easy words and pictures) could be used to communicate this most effectively to clients.
- A structure for initial meetings with client and referrer, including paperwork, can be helpful. This might include a list of information to gather and points to discuss before the therapist and client make a decision together about an assessment (e.g. a summary of the client's life history including bereavement and loss; specific diagnoses that would be helpful to know about; what is happening in the client's life at the moment; support structures available to them to support the process of therapy; has the client had previous therapy treatment).
- Within the client's network, consider who should be notified about the referral, assessment or treatment (e.g. colleagues, a local community team, a GP, family or carers), and how they should be notified. Issues of confidentiality might need to be considered when liaising with professionals and carers.
- It is usual practice to provide assessment and progress reports. Therapists might wish to consider putting the key points from the reports into an accessible format for clients.

The process of therapy

- The issue of consent, both to treatment and to audio/videotaping (if this is appropriate) may need to be addressed at various stages of the therapy.
- An initial appointment (a one-off meeting) in the therapy room can be useful prior to regular sessions beginning, to allow the client to see the setting and have an experience of what will happen there.
- An assessment period allows the therapist and client to think about whether music therapy is suitable at this time. Group or individual treatment, long- or short-term work, or another form of treatment can be considered during the assessment.
- Detailed process notes are usually written after each session. These might include a chronological account of what happened in the session and the therapist's own thoughts and feelings, as well as musical notation and references to illustrative records.
- It can be useful to review the work at set stages, in order to keep developing a picture of the client's life and what they need in order to

progress in therapy. Aims for the music therapy are also useful in order to evaluate the work.

- Keep clients and carers informed of possible future plans for treatment. This can partly be managed through a review meeting built into a series of sessions, to discuss with the client and maybe family/carers what could happen next.
- Endings are important and can be prepared for in different ways, using accessible materials to count down sessions, and allowing time for the ending to be understood.

Professional issues

- Music therapists may find it useful to develop networks with music therapy colleagues in their geographical area.
- Continuing professional development (CPD) meetings such as special interest groups are stimulating and thought provoking to attend.
- Regular clinical supervision with a qualified, registered supervisor with appropriate experience gives opportunities to think in depth about music therapy clinical work.
- CPD needs are usefully discussed with a manager and supervisor (perhaps at appraisal), and appropriate training and development opportunities considered.
- Therapists working with adults with learning disabilities will need to consider child protection and vulnerable adult policies in their area (see DOH 2003a; DOH and Home Office 2000).

Working with people with profound disabilities

- The instruments offered to clients with profound disabilities need particular qualities. Small, hand-held instruments that sound easily are useful, as well as larger freestanding instruments that can be positioned near to a client (perhaps on a boom stand). The sensitive introduction of adapted beaters and instruments can be useful.
- Therapists should have awareness of the importance of responding to tiny sounds, providing an appropriate musical environment when the client is silent, and responding to material other than music (facial expression, body language, or movements such as rocking).
- The environment that will be offered to these clients needs careful consideration. Will clients find it easier to play seated, in their wheelchair, or on a mat or beanbag?
- Think about working in a group setting with another therapist or worker. Music therapists embarking on group work alone might consider working with a small group or three or four clients.

- Explore ways to sustain the work (e.g. seek adequate supervision from a suitably experienced music therapist and further specialist training).
- Collaborate with other professionals to gain information and expertise regarding physical and communication ability (e.g. physiotherapists and speech and language therapists).
- Consider providing staff training for staff, to develop staff knowledge about music therapy and to support the capacity of staff to respond sensitively to clients who have severe barriers to communication. Music therapy workshops, supervision of music-based groups and intensive interaction training could be offered.
- Consider ways to liaise with carers and families (e.g. send information sheets about music therapy, and try to meet with carers and families at reviews). A client's carers or family may not know anything about the work that is being undertaken in music therapy if they are not informed by the therapist.

Useful organizations and websites

Legislation and guidance

Valuing People. A New Strategy for Learning Disability for the 21st Century, London: DOH (2001)
Website: www.dh.gov.uk

The Same as You? A Review of Services for People with Learning Disabilities, Edinburgh: Scottish Executive (1999)
Website: www.scotland.gov.uk/Home

Fulfilling the Promises: Proposals for a Framework for Services for People with Learning Disabilities, Wales: Learning Disability Advisory Group (2000)
Website: www.wales.gov.uk/assemblydata

Disability Discrimination Act, London: HMSO (1995, updated 2005)
Website: www.drc-gb.org/thelaw/thedda.asp

The Children Act Guidance and Regulations, London: Department of Health (2004)
Website: www.opsi.gov.uk/acts/acts2004/20040031.htm

National Health Service and Community Care Act, London: Department of Health (1990)
Website: www.opsi.gov.uk/acts/acts1990/Ukpga_19900019_en_1.htm

Human Rights Act, London: HSMO (1998, implemented 2000)
Website: www.opsi.gov.uk/acts/acts1998/19980042.htm

Carers (Equal Oppportunities) Act, London: DOH (2004)
Website: www.opsi.gov.uk/acts/acts2004/20040015.htm

National Health Service (NHS) information
Website: www.nhs.uk

Department of Health (DOH)
Website: www.dh.gov.uk

Department of Health, Social Services and Public Safety (DHSSPS)
Website: www.dhsspsni.gov.uk

Support and information groups/websites

Batten Disease Family Association
Website: www.bdfa-uk.org.uk/

British Epilepsy Association
Website: www.epilepsy.org.uk
Tel: 0808 800 5050

British Institute of Learning Disabilities (BILD)
Website: www.bild.org.uk
Tel: 01562 723010

Carers UK
Website: www.carersuk.org
Tel: 020 7490 8818/0808 808 7777

Challenging Behaviour Foundation
Website: www.thecbf.org.uk
Tel: 01634 838739

Down's Syndrome Association
Website: www.downs-syndrome.org.uk or www.dsa-uk.org.com
Tel: 0845 230 0372

Easy info
Website: http://www.easyinfo.org.uk

Foundation for People with Learning Disabilities
Website: www.learningdisabilities.org.uk
Tel: 020 7803 1100

Fragile X Society
Website: www.fragilex.org.uk
Tel: 01371 875100

International Autistic Research Organisation
Website: www.charitynet.org/~iaro
Tel: 020 8777 0095

Learning about Intellectual Disabilities and Health
Website: www.intellectualdisability.info/home.htm
Tel: 020 8725 5496

Makaton Vocabulary Development Project
Website: www.makaton.org
Tel: 01276 61390

Mencap
Website: www.mencap.org.uk
Tel: 0808 808 1111 (minicom 0808 808 8181)

Mind
Website: www.mind.org.uk
Tel: 020 8519 2122/0845 766 0163

National Autistic Society
Website: www.nas.org.uk
Tel: 0845 070 4004

National Development Team
Website: www.ndt.org.uk
Tel: 01473 836 440

National Society for Epilepsy
Website: www.epilepsynse.org.uk
Tel: 01494 601300

Respond
Website: www.respond.org.uk
Tel: 020 7383 0700
Helpline: 0808 808 0700

SCOPE (previously named The Spastic Society)
Website: www.scope.org.uk
Tel: 020 7619 7100/0808 800 3333

Sibs (for brothers and sisters of children/adults with special needs)
Website: www.sibs.org.uk
Tel: 01535 645453

Tizard Centre
Website: www.kent.ac.uk/tizard
Tel: 01277 827373/827875

References

Abberley, P. (1992) 'The concept of oppression and the development of a social theory of disability', in T. Booth and W. Swann (eds) *Learning for All (2): Policies for Diversity in Education*, Buckingham: Open University Press, 231–246.

Agrotou, A. (1998) 'Psychodynamic group music therapy with profoundly learning disabled residents and their carers: developing a theory and practice for the realisation of therapeutic aims for residents and the acquirement of therapist's skills by carers', unpublished doctoral thesis, University of Sheffield.

Agrotou, A. (1999) *Sounds and Meaning: Group Music Therapy with People with Profound Learning Difficulties and their Carers*, London: Lumiere.

Alaszewski, A. (1988) 'From villains to victims', in A. Leighton (ed.) *Mental Handicap in the Community*, London: Woodhead-Faulkner, 3–13.

Aldridge, D. and Aldridge, G. (1992) 'Two epistemologies: music therapy and medicine in the treatment of dementia', *The Arts in Psychotherapy*, 19: 243–255.

Aldridge, D., Brandt, G. and Wohler, D. (1990) 'Perspective – toward a common language among the creative art therapies', *The Arts in Psychotherapy*, 17: 189–195.

Alperson, P. (2002) 'Introduction: diversity and community', in P. Alperson (ed.) *Diversity and Community. An Interdisciplinary Reader*, Boston: Blackwell, 1–30.

Alvarez, A. (2002) *Live Company – Psychoanalytic Psychotherapy with Autistic, Borderline, Deprived and Abused Children*, Hove, UK: Brunner-Routledge.

Alvin, J. (1975) *Music Therapy*, London: Hutchinson.

Alvin, J. and Warwick, A. (1992) *Music Therapy for the Autistic Child*, Oxford: Oxford University Press.

American Psychiatric Association (APA, 1994) *Diagnostic and Statistical Manual of Mental Disorders (DSM-IV)*, Washington DC: America Psychiatric Association.

Amit, V. (ed.) (2002) *Realizing Community. Concepts, Social Relationships and Sentiments*, London: Routledge, 1–20.

Ansdell, G. (1995) *Music for Life. Aspects of Creative Music Therapy with Adult Clients*, London: Jessica Kingsley Publishers.

Ansdell, G. (2002) 'Community music therapy and the winds of change – a discussion paper', in B. Stige (ed.) *Contemporary Voices in Music Therapy. Communication, Culture, and Community*, Norway: Unipub Forlag, 109–142.

Ansdell, G. and Pavlicevic, M. (2001) *Beginning Research in the Arts Therapies. A Practical Guide*, London: Jessica Kingsley Publishers.

Arthur, A. (1999) 'Using staff consultation to facilitate the emotional development of adults with learning disabilities', *British Journal of Learning Disabilities*, 27: 93–98.

Arthur, A (2003) 'The emotional lives of people with learning disability', *British Journal of Learning Disabilities*, 31: 25–30.

Aspis, S. (2002) 'Self-advocacy for people with learning difficulties', in B. Bytheway, V. Bacigalupos, J. Bornat, J. Johnson and S. Spurr (eds) *Understanding Care, Welfare and Community. A Reader*, London: Routledge, 255–262.

Atkinson, C. (2003) 'The longest goodbye – a case study', *British Journal of Music Therapy*, 17(2): 90–96.

Attwood, T. (1998) *Asperger's Syndrome*, London: Jessica Kingsley Publishers.

August, G.J., Stewart, M.A. and Tsai, L. (1981) 'The incidence of cognitive disabilities in the siblings of autistic children', *British Journal of Psychiatry*, 138: 416–422.

Ayres, A.J. (1979) *Sensory Integration and the Child*, Los Angeles: Western Psychological Services.

Barnes, B., Ernst, S. and Hyde, K. (1999) *An Introduction to Groupwork. A Group-Analytic Approach Basic Texts in Counselling and Psychotherapy*, Basingstoke: Macmillan.

Baron-Cohen, S. (1995) *Mindblindness: An Essay on Autism and Theory of Mind*, Cambridge, MA: MIT Press.

Baron-Cohen, S., Leslie, A.M. and Frith, U. (1985) 'Does the autistic child have a "theory of mind"?', *Cognition*, 21: 37–46.

Barron, D. (1989) 'Slings and arrows', in D. Brandon (ed.) *Mutual Respect. Therapeutic Approaches to Working with People who have Learning Difficulties*, Croydon: Hexagon, 17–25.

Bates, R. (1992) 'Psychotherapy with people with learning difficulties', in A. Waitman and S. Conboy-Hill (eds) *Psychotherapy and Mental Handicap*, London: Sage, 81–98.

Bauman, Z. (2001) *Community. Seeking Safety in an Insecure World*, Bristol: The Polity Press/Blackwell.

Bayley, M. (1997a) 'Empowering and relationships', in P. Ramcharan, G. Roberts, G. Grant and J. Borland (eds) *Empowerment in Everyday Life*, London: Jessica Kingsley Publishers, 15–34.

Bayley, M. (1997b) *What Price Friendship? Encouraging the Relationships of People with Learning Difficulties*, Croydon: Hexagon.

Beail, N. (1989) 'Understanding emotions', in D. Brandon (ed.) *Mutual Respect. Therapeutic Approaches to Working with People who have Learning Difficulties*, Croydon: Hexagon, 27–45.

Bell, D.M. and Espie, C.A. (2002) 'A preliminary investigation into staff satisfaction, staff emotions and attitudes in a unit for men with learning disabilities and serious challenging behaviours', *British Journal of Learning Disabilities*, 30(1): 19–27.

Berger, D.S. (2002) *Music Therapy, Sensory Integration and the Autistic Child*, London: Jessica Kingsley Publishers.

Berrios, G. (1994) 'Mental illness and mental retardation: history and concepts', in N. Bowas (ed.) *Mental Health in Mental Retardation*, Cambridge: Cambridge University Press.

Bettelheim, B. (1967) *The Empty Fortress: Infantile Autism and the Birth of the Self*, New York: Free Press.

Bion, W.R. (1961) *Experiences in Groups*, London: Tavistock.

Bion, W.R. (1962a) *Learning from Experience*, London: Maresfield.

Bion, W.R. (1962b) *Second Thoughts*, London: Karnac.

Blackburn, R. (1992) 'On music therapy, fairy tales and endings', *Journal of British Music Therapy*, 6(1): 5–9.

Boal, A. (1995) *The Rainbow of Desire. The Boal Method of Theatre and Therapy*, London: Routledge.

Bowlby, J. (1973) *Attachment and Loss, Volume Two: Separation*, London: Hogarth Press.

Bowlby, J. (1979) *The Making and Breaking of Affectional Bonds*, London: Tavistock.

Bowlby, J. (1988) *A Secure Base: Clinical Applications of Attachment Theory*, London and New York: Routledge.

Bradshaw, J. (2001) 'Communication partnerships with people with profound and multiple learning disabilities', *Tizard Learning Disability Review*, 6(2): 6–15.

Brechin, A. (1988) 'Personal relationships and personal fulfilment', in A. Leighton (ed.) *Mental Handicap in the Community*, London: Woodhead-Faulkner, 110–125.

Brown, H. and Smith, H. (1992) 'Inside out: a psychodynamic approach to normalisation', in H. Brown and H. Smith (eds) *Normalisation: A reader for the Nineties*, London: Routledge, 84–99.

Brown, S. (1994) 'Autism and music therapy – is change possible, and why music?', *Journal of British Music Therapy*, 8(1): 15–25.

Brownell, M.D. (2002) 'Musically adapted social stories to modify behaviours in students with autism: four case studies', *Journal of Music Therapy*, 39(2): 117–144.

Bruscia, K. (1987) *Improvisational Models of Music Therapy*, Springfield: Charles C. Thomas.

Bruscia, K. (1995) 'The process of doing qualitative research', in B. Wheeler (ed.) *Music Therapy Research. Quantitative and Qualitative Perspectives*, Gilsum, NH: Barcelona Publishers, 401–443.

Bruscia, K.E. (2002) 'Foreword', in B. Stige (ed.) *Culture Centred Music Therapy*, Gilsum, NH: Barcelona Publishers.

Bryan, A. (1989) 'Autistic group case study', *Journal of British Music Therapy*, 3(1): 16–21.

Bunt, L. (1994) *Music Therapy. An Art Beyond Words*, London: Routledge.

Bunt, L. (1997) 'Clinical and therapeutic uses of music', in D.J. Hargreaves and A.C. North (eds) *The Social Psychology of Music*, Oxford: Oxford University Press, 249–267.

Cabinet Office (2005) *Improving the Life Chances of Disabled People*, London: Cabinet Office.

Casement, P. (1985) *On Learning From the Patient*, London: Tavistock.

Chazan, R. (2001) *The Group as Therapist*, London: Routledge.

Chesner, A. (1995) 'The use of fairytales in group dramatherapy: a dramatherapy and music therapy collaboration', in A. Chesner *Dramatherapy for People with Learning Disabilities*, London: Jessica Kingsley Publishers, 158–190.

Clarkson, G. (1991) 'Music therapy for a nonverbal autistic adult', in K.E. Bruscia (ed.) *Case Studies in Music Therapy*, Gilsum, NH: Barcelona Publishers, 373–385.

Clough, J. (1992) 'Music therapy: a description of work with a mentally handicapped young man', *Journal of British Music Therapy*, 6(2): 16–23.

Coleman, M. and Gillberg, C. (1985) *The Biology of the Autistic Syndromes*, New York: Praeger.

Collins, S. (1999) 'Treatment and therapeutic interventions: psychological approaches', *Tizard Learning Disability Review*, 4(2): 20–27.

Cooper, S.-A. (2003) 'Classification and assessment of psychiatric disorders in people with learning disabilities', *Psychiatry*, August: 12–17.

Community Care Development Centre/Judith Trust (2002) *Include Us Too. Developing and Improving Services to Meet the Mental Health Needs of People with Learning Disabilities. A Workbook for Commissioners and Managers in Mental Health and Learning Disability Services*, London: Kings College.

Cowan, J. (1989) 'Role limits in music therapy', *Journal of British Music Therapy*, 3(1): 5–9.

Dalal, F. (2002) *Race, Colour and the Process of Racialization – New Perspectives from Group Analysis, Psychoanalysis and Sociology*, London and New York: Brunner-Routledge, 111–119.

Darnley-Smith, R. and Patey, H. (2003) *Music Therapy*, London: Sage.

Davies, A. and Richards, E. (eds) (2002) *Music Therapy and Group Work – Sound Company*, London: Jessica Kingsley Publishers.

Davies, A. and Mitchell, A.R.K. (1990) 'Music therapy and elective mutism: a case discussion', *Journal of British Music Therapy*, 4(2): 10–14.

Department of Health (1990) *NHS and Community Care Act*, London: HMSO.

Department of Health (1993) *The Mansell Report*, London: HMSO.

Department of Health (1998) *Signposts for Success in Commissioning and Providing Health Services for People with Learning Disabilities*, London: DOH.

Department of Health (2001a) *Consent. A Guide for People with Learning Disabilities*, London: DOH.

Department of Health (2001b) *Good Practice in Consent Implementation Guide: Consent to Examination or Treatment*, London: DOH.

Department of Health (2001c) *Valuing People. A New Strategy for Learning Disability for the 21st Century*, London: DOH.

Department of Health (2002) *Health Action Plans and Health Facilitation*, London: DOH.

Department of Health (2003a) *Confidentiality NHS Code of Practice*, London: DOH.

Department of Health (2003b) *What to Do if You're Worried a Child is being Abused*, London: DOH.

Department of Health (2005a) *Mental Capacity Act 2005 A Summary*, DOH Website.

Department of Health (2005b) *Records Management NHS Code of Practice*, London: DOH.

Department of Health (2006) *Our Health, Our Care, Our Say, A New Direction for Community Services*, London: DOH.

Department of Health and Home Office (2000) *No Secrets. Guidance on Developing and Implementing Multi-agency Policies and Procedures to Protect Vulnerable Adults from Abuse*, London: DOH.

Department of Health and Social Security (1971) *Better Services for the Mentally Handicapped*, London: HMSO.

Di Franco, G. (2002) 'Music and autism – vocal improvisation as containment of stereotypies', in T. Wigram and J. De Backer (eds) *Clinical Applications of Music Therapy in Developmental Disability, Paediatrics and Neurology*, London: Jessica Kingsley Publishers.

Duffy, B. and Fuller, R. (2000) 'Role of music therapy in social skills development in children with moderate intellectual disability', *Journal of Applied Research in Intellectual Disabilities*, 13(2): 77–89.

Dumbleton, P. (1998) 'Words and numbers', *British Journal of Learning Disability*, 26: 151–153.

Durham, C. (2002) 'Music therapy and neurology', in L. Bunt and S. Hoskyns (eds) *The Handbook of Music Therapy*, London: Brunner-Routledge, 115–131.

Dury, I. (1981) 'Spasticus Autisticus' on *Lord Upminster*, UK: Polydor Records.

Dye, L., Hendy, S.H. and Burton, M. (2004) 'Capacity to consent to participate in research – a recontextualization', *British Journal of Learning Disabilities*, 32(3): 144–150.

Eaton, M.M. (2002) 'The role of art in sustaining communities', in P. Alperson (ed.) *Diversity and Community. An Interdisciplinary Reader*, Boston: Blackwell, 249–264.

Edwards, J. (2002) 'Using the evidence based medicine framework to support music therapy posts in health care settings', *British Journal of Music Therapy*, 16(1): 29–34.

Edwards, J. (2005) 'Possibilities and problems for evidence based practice in music therapy', *The Arts in Psychotherapy*, 32(4): 293–301.

Eisler, J. (1993) 'Stretto-music therapy in the context of the multidisciplinary team: establishing a place in the multidisciplinary team', *Journal of British Music Therapy* 7(1): 23–24.

Eliatamby, A. and Hampton K. (2001) *Using Values To Change Learning Disability Services*, London: Office for Public Management.

Emerson, E. (1992) 'What is normalization?', in H. Brown and H. Smith (eds) *Normalisation. A Reader for the Nineties*, London: Routledge, 1–18.

Emerson, E. (1995) *Challenging Behaviour: Analysis and Intervention in People with Learning Disabilities*, Cambridge: Cambridge University Press.

Emerson, E. (2004) 'Deinstitutionalisation in England', *Journal of Intellectual and Developmental Disability*, 29: 17–22.

Emerson, E., Hatton, C., Felce, D. and Murphy, G. (2001) *Learning Disabilities. The Fundamental Facts*, London: Foundation for People with Learning Disabilities.

Emerson, E., Hatton, C., Thompson, T. and Parmenter, T.R. (2004) *The International Handbook of Applied Research in Intellectual Disabilities*, Chichester: Wiley.

Emerson, E., Malam, S., Davies, I. and Spencer, K. (2005) *Adults with Learning Difficulties in England 2003/2004*, London: NHS: Health and Social Care Information Centre.

Esquirol, E. (1838) *'Des maladies mentales considerees sous les rapports medical, hygienique et medico-legal'*, cited in G. Berrios 'Mental illness and mental retardation: history and concepts', in N. Bouras (ed.) *Mental Health in Mental Retardation*, Cambridge: Cambridge University Press.

Felce, D. and Perry, J. (1994) *Quality of Life: Its Definition and Measurement*, Cardiff: Welsh Centre for Learning Disabilities Applied Research Unit.

Fillingham, C.L. (2003) 'Relationships and quality of life: examining the issues for adults with learning disabilities in group music therapy', unpublished MA thesis, University of Surrey Roehampton.

Finlay, C., Bruce, H., Magee, W.L., Farrelly, S. and McKenzie, S. (2001) 'How I use music in therapy', *Speech Therapy in Practice*, Autumn: 30–35.

Firth, H. and Rapley, M. (1990) *From Acquaintance to Friendship: Issues for people with Learning Disabilities*, Kidderminster: BIMH Publications.

Fischer, R. (1991) 'Original song drawings in the treatment of a developmentally disabled autistic adult', in K.E. Bruscia (ed.) *Case Studies in Music Therapy*, Gilsum, NH: Barcelona Publishers, 359–371.

Fitton, P. (1994) *Listen to Me*, London: Jessica Kingsley Publishers.

Folstein, S. and Rutter, M. (1977) 'Infantile autism: a genetic study of 21 twin pairs', *Journal of Child Psychology and Psychiatry*, 18: 297–321.

Fonagy, P. (2001) *Attachment Theory and Psychoanalysis*, New York: Other Books.

Foulkes, S.H. (1986) *Group Analytic Psychotherapy. Method and Principles*, London: Karnac.

Foulkes, S.H. and Anthony, E.J. (1984) *Group Psychotherapy: The Psychoanalytic Approach*, London: Karnac.

Foundation for People with Learning Disabilities (2002) *Count Us In. The Report of the Committee of Inquiry into Meeting the Mental Health Needs of Young People with Learning Disabilities*, London: Mental Health Foundation.

Frith, U. (1991) *Autism and Aspergers Syndrome*, Cambridge: Cambridge University Press.

Frith, U. (2003) *Autism. Explaining the Enigma*, Oxford: Blackwell.

Frith, U. and Hill, E. (2004) *Autism: Mind and Brain*, Oxford: Oxford University Press.

Gale, C.P. (1989) 'The question of music therapy with mentally handicapped adults', *Journal of British Music Therapy*, 3(2): 20–30.

Glyn, J. (2002) 'Drummed out of mind', in A. Davies and E. Richards (eds) *Music Therapy and Group Work, Sound Company*, London: Jessica Kingsley Publishers, 43–62.

Goldstein-Roca, S. and Crisafulli, T. (1994) 'Integrative creative arts therapy: a brief treatment model', *The Arts in Psychotherapy*, 21(3): 219–222.

Graham, J. (2004) 'Communicating with the uncommunicative: music therapy with pre-verbal adults', *British Journal of Learning Disabilities*, 32(1): 24–29.

Grant, R.E. (1995) 'Music therapy assessment for developmentally disabled clients', in T. Wigram, B. Saperston and R. West (eds) *The Art and Science of Music Therapy: A Handbook*, London: Harwood, 273–287.

Gray, J. (2002) 'Community as place-making', in V. Amit (ed.) *Realizing Community. Concepts, Social Relationships and Sentiments*, London: Routledge, 38–59.

Grove, N., Bunning, K., Porter, J. and Morgan, M. (2000) *See What I Mean.*

Guidelines to Aid Understanding of Communication by People with Severe and Profound Learning Disabilities, Kidderminster: Bild and Mencap.

Happe, F. (1999) *Autism – an introduction to psychological theory*, Hove, UK: Psychology Press.

Hare, D.J. and Leadbeater, C. (1998) 'Specific factors in assessing and intervening in cases of self-injury by people with autistic conditions', *Journal of Learning Disabilities for Nursing, Health and Social Care*, 2: 60–65.

Hartland-Rowe, L. (2001) 'An exploration of severe learning disability in adults and the study of early interaction', *International Journal of Infant Observation*, 4(3): 42–62.

Heal, M. (1994) 'The development of symbolic function in a young woman with Down's syndrome', in D. Dokter (ed.) *Arts Therapies and Clients with Eating Disorders. Fragile Board*, London: Jessica Kingsley Publishers, 279–294.

Heal-Hughes, M. (1995) 'A comparison of mother–infant interactions and the client–therapist relationship in music therapy sessions', in T. Wigram, B. Saperston and R. West (eds) *The Art and Science of Music Therapy: A Handbook*, London: Harwood, 296–306.

Herman, J. (1992) *Trauma and Recovery*, New York: Basic Books.

Hernandez-Halton, I., Hodges, S., Miller, L. and Simpson, D. (2000) 'A psychotherapy service for children, adolescents and adults with learning disabilities at the Tavistock Clinic, London, UK', *British Journal of Learning Disabilities*, 28: 120–124.

Hewett, D. and Nind, M. (1994) *Access to Communication*, London: David Fulton.

Hewett, D. and Nind, M. (1998) *Interaction in Action: Reflections on the Use of Intensive Interaction*, London: David Fulton.

Hills, B., Norman, I. and Forster, L. (2000) 'A study of burnout and multi-disciplinary team-working amongst professional music therapists', *British Journal of Music Therapy*, 14(1): 32–40.

HMSO (1979) *Jay Report. Report of the Committee of Enquiry into Mental Handicap Nursing and Care*, London: HMSO.

HMSO (1998) *Human Rights Act 1998*, London: HMSO.

Ho, A. (2004) 'To be labelled, or not to be labelled: that is the question', in *British Journal of Learning Disabilities*, 32(2): 86–92.

Hobson, P. (2002) *The Cradle of Thought*, London: Macmillan.

Hodges, S. (2003) *Counselling Adults with Learning Disabilities*, Basingstoke: Palgrave Macmillan.

Hollins, S. (1993–2005) *Books Without Words Series*, London: St George's Hospital Medical School.

Hollins, S. (1997) 'Quality of life and personal meaning', paper presented at *Living Fully*, London: St George's Hospital Medical School, University of London.

Hollins, S. (2000) Developmental psychiatry – insights from learning disability', *British Journal of Psychiatry*, 177: 201–206.

Hollins, S. and Evered, C. (1990) 'Group process and content: the challenge of mental handicap', *Group Analysis*, 23: 55–67.

Hollins, S. and Sinason, V. (2000) 'Psychotherapy, learning disabilities and trauma: new perspectives', *British Journal of Psychiatry*, 176: 32–36.

Holt, R. (1995) 'Occupational stress', in L. Goldberger and S. Breznitz (eds)

Handbook of Stress: Theoretical and Clinical Aspects, New York: Free Press, 419–444.

Hooper, J. (1993) 'Developing interaction through shared musical experiences: a strategy to enhance and validate the descriptive approach', in M. Heal and T. Wigram (eds) *Music Therapy in Health and Education*, London: Jessica Kingsley Publishers, 208–213.

Hooper, J. (2001) 'An introduction to vibroacoustic therapy and an examination of its place in music therapy practice', *British Journal of Music Therapy*, 15(2): 69–77.

Hooper, J. (2002) 'Using music to develop peer interaction: an examination of the response of two subjects with a learning disability', *British Journal of Learning Disabilities*, 30(4): 166–170.

Hooper, J. and Lindsay, B. (1990) 'Music and the mentally handicapped – the effect of music on anxiety', *British Journal of Music Therapy*, 4(2): 19–26.

Hooper, J., Lindsay, B. and Richardson, I. (1991) 'Recreation and music therapy: an experimental study', *British Journal of Music Therapy*, 15(2): 11.

Hooper, J., McManus, A. and McIntyre, A. (2004) 'Exploring the link between music therapy and sensory integration: an individual case study', *British Journal of Music Therapy*, 18(1): 15–23.

Jacobs, A. (2000) *An Investigation into the Perception of Music Therapy in a Service for Adults with Learning Disabilities – The Way Forward*. Internet page at URL: http//www.apu.ac.uk/music/mt-research/dissertations/jacobs.html (accessed 16/03/2004).

Jensen, B. (1999) 'Music therapy with psychiatric in-patients: a case study with a young schizophrenic man', in T. Wigram and J. De Backer (eds) *Clinical Applications of Music Therapy in Psychiatry*, London: Jessica Kingsley Publishers, 44–60.

John, D. (1992) 'Towards music psychotherapy', *Journal of British Music Therapy*, 6(1): 10–13.

John, D. (1993) 'The therapeutic relationship in music therapy as a tool in the treatment of psychosis', in Wigram, T. (ed.) *The Art and Science of Music Therapy*, Chur: Harwood, 157–166.

Jones, A.M. and Bonnar, S. (1996) 'Group psychotherapy with learning disabled adults', *British Journal of Learning Disabilities*, 24: 65–69.

Jones, P. (2005) *The Arts Therapies. A Revolution in Healthcare*, Hove, UK: Brunner-Routledge.

Kanner, L. (1973) *Childhood Psychosis: Initial Studies and New Insights*, Washington, DC: Winston.

Kellett, M. and Nind, M. (2001) 'Ethics in quasi-experimental research on people with severe learning disabilities: dilemmas and compromises', *British Journal of Learning Disabilities*, 29: 51–55.

Kennelly, J., Hamilton, L. and Cross, J. (2001) 'The interface of music therapy and speech pathology in the rehabilitation of children with acquired brain injury', *Australian Journal of Music Therapy*, 12: 13–20.

Kenny, C. and Stige, B. (2002) *Contemporary Voices in Music Therapy. Communication, Culture, and Community*, Oslo: Unipub.

Kevan, F. (2003) 'Challenging behaviour and communication difficulties', *British Journal of Learning Disabilities*, 31(2): 75–80.

Kiernan, C. (1999) 'Participation in research by people with learning disability: origins and issues', *British Journal of Learning Disabilities*, 27: 43–47.

Klotz, J. (2004) 'Sociocultural study of intellectual disability: moving beyond labeling and social constructionist perspectives', *British Journal of Learning Disabilities*, 32(2): 93–104.

Kushlik, A., Trower, P. and Dagnan, D. (1997) 'Applying cognitive behavioural approaches to the carers of people with learning disabilities who display challenging behaviour', in B. Stenfert Kroese, D. Dagna and K. Loudvidis (eds) *Cognitive-Behaviour Therapy for People with Learning Disabilities*, London: Routledge, 141–161.

Lacey, P. and Ouvry, C. (eds) (1998) *People with Profound and Multiple Learning Disabilities. A Collaborative Approach to Meeting Complex Needs*, London: David Fulton.

Lally, J. (1993) 'Staff issues: training, support and management', in I. Fleming and B. Stenfert Kroese (eds) *People with Learning Disabilities and Severe Challenging Behaviour. Advances in Research, Service Delivery and Interventions*, Manchester: Manchester University Press, 141–163.

Lapping, A.J. (2003) 'I see it feelingly . . . look with thine ears – an investigation into the perception of emotional expression in music therapy with clients with severe learning disability', unpublished MA thesis, University of Surrey Roehampton.

Lawson, W. (2001) *Understanding and Working with the Spectrum of Autism*, London: Jessica Kingsley Publishers.

Leaning, B. and Watson, T. (2006) 'From the inside looking out – an intensive interaction group for people with profound and multiple learning disabilities', *British Journal of Learning Disabilities*, 34(2): 103–109.

Levinge, A. (2002) 'Supervision or double vision. An exploration of the task of music therapy supervision', *British Journal of Music Therapy*, 16(2): 83–89.

Lovett, H. (1996) *Learning to Listen: Positive Approaches and People with Difficult Behaviour*, Baltimore: Paul H. Brookes.

McCarthy, J. (2001) 'Post-traumatic stress disorder in people with a learning disability', *Advances in Psychiatric Treatment*, 7: 163–169.

McCarthy, M. (1998) 'Interviewing people with learning disabilities about sensitive topics: a discussion of ethical issues', *British Journal of Learning Disabilities*, 26: 140–145.

McConkey, R. (1998) 'Life in society: community integration', in W. Fraser, D. Sines and M. Kerr (eds) *Hallas' The Care of People with Intellectual Disabilities*, London: Hodder Arnold, 71–89.

McGill, P. (2005) 'Models of community care in the UK: past and present', *Learning Disability Review*, 10(1): 46–51.

McIntosh, B. and Whittaker, A. (eds) (1998) *Days of Change*, London: King's Fund.

McIntosh, B. and Whittaker, A. (2000) *Unlocking the Future: Developing New Lifestyles with People who have Complex Disabilities*, London: King's Fund.

McKenzie, K., Mathieson, E., McKaskie, K., Hamilton L. and Murray, G.C. (2000) 'The impact of group training on emotion recognition in individuals with a learning disability', *British Journal of Learning Disabilities*, 28(4): 143–147.

Macleod, F.J., Morrison, F., Swanston, M. and Lindsay, W. (2002) 'Effects of relocation on the communication and challenging behaviour of four people with severe learning disabilities', *British Journal of Learning Disabilities*, 30(1): 32–37.

Malin, N. (1987) *Reassessing Community Care (With Particular Reference to Provision for People with Mental Handicap and for People with Mental Illness)*, London: Croom Helm.

Mattison, V. and Pistrang, N. (2004) 'The ending of relationships', in D. Simpson and L. Miller (eds) *Unexpected Gains: Psychotherapy with People with Learning Disabilities*, London: Karnac.

May, D. (2001) *Transition and Change in the Lives of People with Intellectual Disabilities*, London: Jessica Kingsley Publishers.

Mayo, M. (2000) *Cultures, Communities, Identities. Cultural Strategies for Participation and Empowerment*, Basingstoke: Palgrave Macmillan.

Mencap (2002) *Making it Work*, London: Mencap.

Mir, G., Nocon, A., Ahmad, W. and Jones, L. (2001) *Learning Difficulties and Ethnicity*, London: DOH.

Moss, H. (1999) 'Creating a new music therapy post', *British Journal of Music Therapy*, 13(2): 49–58.

Murphy, G. (1994) 'Understanding challenging behaviour', in E. Emerson, P. McGill and J. Mansell (eds) *Severe Learning Disabilities and Challenging Behaviours: Designing High Quality Services*, London: Chapman and Hall.

Murphy, G.H., Oliver, C., Corbett, J., Crayton, L., Hales, J., Head, D. and Hall, S. (1993) 'Epidemiology of self-injury, characteristics of people with severe self-injury and initial treatment outcome', in C. Kiernan (ed.) *Research to Practice? Implications of Research on the Challenging Behaviour of People with Learning Disabilities*, Clevedon: BILD.

Nadirshaw, Z. (1997) 'Cultural issues', in J. O'Hara and A. Sperlinger (eds) *Adults with Learning Disabilities, A Practical Approach for Health Professionals*, Chichester: Wiley, 139–153.

Nordoff, P. and Robbins, C. (1971) *Therapy in Music for Handicapped Children*, London: Gollancz.

Nygaard Pederson, I. (2002) 'Analytical music therapy with adults in mental health and counselling work', in J.T. Eschen (ed.) *Analytical Music Therapy*, London: Jessica Kingsley Publishers, 64–84.

O'Brien, J. (1987) 'A guide to lifestyle planning: using the activities catalogue to integrate services and natural support systems', in B. Wilcox and G.T. Bellamy (eds) *A Comprehensive Guide to the Activities Catalogue: Alternative Curriculum for Youth Adults with Severe Disabilities*, Baltimore: Paul H. Brookes.

O'Brien, J. (1992) 'Developing high quality services for people with developmental disabilities', in V. Bradley and H. Bersani (eds) *Quality Assurance for Individuals with Developmental Disabilities*, Baltimore: Paul H. Brookes, 17–31.

O'Brien, J. (2005) 'A turning point in the struggle to replace institutions', *Learning Disability Review*, 10(1): 12–17.

O'Connor, H. (2001) 'Will we grow out of it? A psychotherapy group for people with learning disabilities', *Psychodynamic Counselling*, 7: 297–314.

Odell, H. (1979) 'Music therapy in SSN hospitals, report of BSMT meeting', *British Journal of Music Therapy*, 10(4): 12–15.

Odell-Miller, H. (1993) 'Stretto. Working with a multidisciplinary team – music therapy in the context of the multidisciplinary team', *Journal of British Music Therapy*, 7: 24–25.

Odell-Miller, H. (2002) 'One man's journey and the importance of time: music therapy in an NHS mental health day centre', in A. Davies and E. Richards (eds) *Music Therapy and Group Work, Sound Company*, London: Jessica Kingsley Publishers, 63–76.

Odell-Miller, H. and Darnley-Smith, R. (2001) 'Historical perspectives interview series. Helen Odell-Miller interviewed by Rachel Darnley-Smith', *British Journal of Music Therapy*, 15(1): 8–13.

Ogden, T.H. (2004) *The Primitive Edge of Experience*, Lanham, MD: Rowman and Littlefield.

O'Hara, J. and Sperlinger, A. (1997) *Adults with Learning Disabilities*, Chichester: Wiley.

Oldfield, A. (2005) 'Information from my PhD regarding the music therapy diagnostic assessments (MTDA)', unpublished thesis.

Oldfield, A. (undated) 'Music therapy as a contribution to the diagnosis made by the staff team in child and family psychiatry – an initial description of a methodology', in T. Wigram (ed.) *Assessment and Evaluation in the Arts Therapies: Art Therapy, Music Therapy and Dramatherapy*, Radlett: Harper House.

Oldfield, A. and Adams, M. (1990) 'The effects of music therapy on a group of profoundly mentally handicapped adults', *Journal of Mental Deficiency Research*, 34(2): 107–125.

Oldfield, A. and Adams, M. (1995) 'The effects of music therapy on a group of adults with profound learning difficulties', in A. Gilroy and C. Lee (eds) *Art and Music: Therapy and Research*, London: Routledge, 164–182.

Oppenheim, A.N. (1992) *Questionnaire Design, Interviewing and Attitude Measurement*, London: Continuum.

Ourvry, C. (1998) 'Making relationships', in P. Lacey and C. Ourvry (eds) *People with Profound and Multiple Learning Disabilities: A Collaborative Approach to Meeting Complex Needs*, Chichester: Wiley, 66–75.

Ovretveit, J. (1993) *Co-ordinating Community Care*, Buckingham: Open University Press.

Pantlin, A.W. (1985) 'Group-analytic psychotherapy with mentally handicapped patients'. *Group Analysis*, 18(1): 44–53.

Patey, H.M. (2000) 'The music therapy profession in modern Britain', in P. Horden (ed.) *Music as Medicine*, London: Ashgate.

Pavlicevic, M. and Ansdell, G. (eds) (2004) *Community Music Therapy*, London: Jessica Kingsley Publishers.

Pelham, G. and Stacy, J. (1999) *Counselling Skills for Creative Arts Therapists*, London: Worth.

Philipson, C., Bernard, M., Phillips, J. and Ogg, J. (2002) 'Social change, networks and family life', in B. Bytheway, V. Bacigalupo, J. Bornat, J. Johnson and S. Spurr (eds) *Understanding Care, Welfare and Community. A Reader*, London: Routledge, 112–120.

Pines, M. (ed.) (1983) *The Evolution of Group Analysis*, London: Jessica Kingsley Publishers.

PMLD Network (2003) *Valuing People with Profound and Multiple Learning*

Disabilities (PMLD), London: Mencap/Foundation for People with Learning Disabilities.

Porter, J., Ouvry, C., Morgan, M. and Downs, C. (2001) 'Interpreting the communication of people with profound and multiple learning difficulties', *British Journal of Learning Disabilities*, 29: 12–16.

Prasher, V. (1999) 'Presentation and management of depression in people with learning disability', *Advances in Psychiatric Treatment*, 5, 447–454.

Prichard, J.C. (1835) *A Treatise on Insanity*, cited in G. Berrios 'Mental illness and mental retardation: history and concepts', in N. Bouras (ed.) *Mental Health in Mental Retardation*, Cambridge: Cambridge University Press.

Priestley, M. (1994) *Essays on Analytical Music Therapy*, Gilsum, NH: Barcelona Publishers.

Race, D.G. (1995) 'Historical development of service provision', in N. Malin (ed.) *Services for People with Learning Disabilities*, London: Routledge.

Race, D.G. (2002) *Learning Disability: A Social Approach*, London: Routledge.

Remington, B. (1998) 'Working with people with communication difficulties', in E. Emerson, C. Hatton, J. Bromley and A. Caine (eds) *Clinical Psychology and People with Intellectual Disabilities*, Chichester: Wiley, 231–244.

Reyes-Simpson, E. (2004) 'When there is too much to take in: some factors that restrict the capacity to think', in D. Simpson and L. Miller (eds) *Unexpected Gains Psychotherapy with People with Learning Disabilities*, London: Karnac.

Richards, E. and Hind, H. (2002) 'Finding a place to play: a music therapy group for adults with learning disabilities', in A. Davies and E. Richards (eds) *Music Therapy and Group Work. Sound Company*, London: Jessica Kingsley Publishers.

Ritchie, F. (1991) 'Behind closed doors; a case study', *Journal of British Music Therapy*, 5(2): 4–10.

Ritchie, F. (1993a) 'Opening doors. The effects of music therapy with people who have severe learning difficulties and display challenging behaviour', in M. Heal and T. Wigram (eds) *Music Therapy in Health and Education*, London: Jessica Kingsley Publishers, 91–102.

Ritchie, F. (1993b) 'Stretto: teaming up, in music therapy in the context of the multidisciplinary team', *Journal of British Music Therapy*, 7(1): 25–26.

Ross, E. and Oliver, C. (2003) 'Preliminary analysis of the psychometric properties of the mood, interest and pleasure questionnaire (MIPQ) for adults with severe and profound learning disabilities', *British Journal of Clinical Psychology*, 42: 81–93.

Royal College of Psychiatrists (2001) *DC-LD: Diagnostic Criteria for Psychiatric Disorders for use with Adults with Learning Disabilities/Mental Retardation*, London: Gaskell.

Rutter, M. (1983) 'Cognitive deficits in the pathogenesis of autism', *Journal of Child Psychology and Psychiatry*, 24: 513–531.

Rutter, M., Macdonald, H., LeCouter, A., Harrington, R., Bolton, P. and Bailey, A. (1990) 'Genetic factors in child psychiatric disorders: II. Empirical findings', *Journal of Child Psychology and Psychiatry*, 31: 39–83.

Ryan, R. (1994) 'Post traumatic stress disorders in people with developmental disabilities', *Community Mental Health Journal*, 30(1): 45–54.

Samuel, J. and Pritchard, M. (2001) 'The ignored minority: meeting the needs of people with profound disability', *Tizard Learning Disability Review*, 6(2): 34–44.

Saul, B. (2004) 'Fulfilling lives. An evaluation of a music therapy service for people with severe learning disability and challenging behaviour in South East London', unpublished MA thesis, London: Roehampton University.

Schalock, R. (1996) *Quality of Life: Volume 1 – Conceptualization and Measurement*, Washington, DC: American Association of Mental Retardation.

Schutzman, M. and Cohen-Cruz, J. (1994) 'Introduction', in M. Schutzman and J. Cohen-Cruz *Playing Boal. Theatre, Therapy, Activism*, London: Routledge, 1–16.

Scottish Executive (2001) *'The Same As You?' – A Review of Services for People with Learning Disabilities*, Edinburgh: Scottish Executive.

Shakespeare, T. (1998) *The Disability Reader*, London: Continuum.

Sheehy, K. and Nind, M. (2005) 'Emotional well-being for all: mental health and people with profound and multiple learning disabilities', *British Journal of Learning Disabilities*, 33: 34–38.

Sheppard, N. (2003) 'Relationship issues: friendships and group dynamics', in S. Hodges (ed.) *Counselling Adults with Learning Disabilities*, Basingstoke: Palgrave Macmillan, 130–147.

Simpson, D. and Miller, L. (2004) *Unexpected Gains. Psychotherapy with People with Learning Disabilities*, London: Karnac.

Sinason, V. (1992) *Mental Handicap and the Human Condition*, London: Free Association Books.

Sinason, V. (1999) 'The psychotherapeutic needs of the learning disabled and multiply disabled child', in M. Lanyado and A. Horne (eds) *The Handbook of Child and Adolescent Psychotherapy*, London: Routledge.

Skelly, A. (2002) 'Valuing people: a critical psychoanalytic perspective in reply to Baum and Webb', *Clinical Psychology*, 18: 42.

Slivka, H. and Magill, H.L. (1986) cited in Decuir, A. (1991) 'Trends in music and family therapy', *The Arts in Psychotherapy*, 18: 195–199.

Smeijsters, H. (1993) 'Music therapy and psychotherapy', *The Arts in Psychotherapy*, 20: 223–229.

Smith, R. (1999) 'Medicine and the marginalised', *British Medical Journal*, 319: 1589–1590.

Sobey, K. (1993) 'Out of sight – out of mind? Reflections on a blind young woman's use of music therapy', *British Journal of Music Therapy*, 7(2): 5–11.

Sobey, K. and Woodcock, J. (1999) 'Psychodynamic music therapy. Considerations in training', in A. Cattanach (ed.) *Process in the Arts Therapies*, London: Jessica Kingsley Publishers.

Steffenberg, S. (1991) 'Neuropsychiatruc assessment of children with autism: a population-based study', *Developmental Medicine and Child Neurology*, 33: 495–511.

Stern, D. (1985) *The Interpersonal World of the Infant: A View from Psychoanalysis and Developmental Psychology*, New York: Basic Books.

Stewart, D. (1996) 'Chaos, noise and a wall of silence: working with primitive affects in psychodynamic group music therapy', *British Journal of Music Therapy*, 10(2): 21–33.

Stewart, D. (2000) 'The state of the UK music therapy profession – personal qualities, working models, support networks and job satisfaction', *British Journal of Music Therapy*, 14(1): 13–31.

Stige, B. (2002) *Culture Centred Music Therapy*, Gilsum, NH: Barcelona Publishers.

Stock Whitaker, D. (2001) *Using Groups to Help People*, 3nd edn, London: Routledge.

Stokes, J. and Sinason, V. (1992) 'Secondary handicap as a defence', in A. Waitman and S. Conboy Hill (eds) *Psychotherapy and Mental Handicap*, London: Sage.

Szatmari, P. and Jones, M.B. (1991) 'IQ and the genetics of autism', *Journal of Child Psychology and Psychiatry*, 32: 897–908.

Szivos, S. (1992) 'The limits to integration?', in H. Brown and H. Smith (eds) *Normalisation. A Reader for the Nineties*, London: Routledge.

Szymanski, L. (1994) 'Mental retardation and mental health: concepts, aetiology and incidence', in N. Bouras (ed.) *Mental Health in Mental Retardation*, Cambridge: Cambridge University Press, 19–33.

Thomas, D. and Woods, H. (2003) *Working with People with Learning Disabilities. Theory and Practice*, London: Jessica Kingsley Publishers.

Thurman, S., Jones, J. and Tarleton, B. (2005) 'Without words – meaningful information for people with high individual communication needs', *British Journal of Learning Disabilities*, 33: 83–89.

Tinbergen, N. and Tinbergen, E.A. (1983) *'Autistic' Children: New Hope for a Cure*, London: Allen and Unwin.

Tizard, J. (1964) *Community Services for the Mentally Handicapped*, Oxford: Oxford University Press.

Toigo, D.A. (1992) 'Autism: integrating a personal perspective with music therapy practice', *Music Therapy Perspectives*, 10(1): 13–20.

Toolan, P. and Coleman, S. (1995) 'Music therapy, a description of process: engagement and avoidance in five people with learning disabilities', *British Journal of Music Therapy*, 9(1): 17–24.

Towell, D. (2004) 'Person-centred planning in the strategy for valuing people', in *BILD Yearbook 2004*, Worcestershire: BILD.

Townsend, B. (2004) 'A sense of musical relatedness and subsequent gains – forming an approach to individual music therapy in adult learning disability', unpublished MA dissertation, Anglia Polytechnic University.

Trevarthen, C. (1993) 'The self born in intersubjectivity: the psychology of an infant communicating', in U. Neisser (ed.) *The Perceived Self*, New York: Cambridge University Press, 121–173.

Trevarthen, C., Robarts, J., Papoudi, D. and Aitken, K. (1998) *Children with Autism. Diagnosis and Intervention to Meet their Needs*, London: Jessica Kingsley Publishers.

Tustin, F. (1986) *Autistic Barriers in Neurotic Patients*, London: Karnac.

Tustin, F. (1992) *Autistic States in Children*, London: Routledge.

Twyford, K. (2004) 'New directions: an investigation into music therapy as part of a collaborative multidisciplinary approach', unpublished MA thesis, University of Roehampton.

Twyford, K. and Watson, T. (in press) *Integrated Team Working, Music Therapy as part of Transdisciplinary and Collaborative Approaches*, London: Jessica Kingsley Publishers.

Tyler, H.M. (1998) 'Behind the mask: an exploration of the true and false self as revealed in music therapy', *British Journal of Music Therapy*, 12(2): 60–66.

Usher, J. (1998) 'Lighting up the mind. Evolving a model of consciousness and its application to improvisation in music therapy', *British Journal of Music Therapy*, 12(1): 4–19.

Vinogradov, S. and Yalom, I. (1989) 'What makes group psychotherapy work?', in S. Vinogradov and I. Yalom *Concise Guide to Group Psychotherapy*, Arlington, VA: America Psychiatric Press, 11–29.

Wager, K.M. (2000) 'The effects of music therapy upon an adult male with autism and mental retardation: a four-year case study', *Music Therapy Perspectives*, 18(2): 131–140.

Walker, A. and Walker, C. (2002) 'Ageing, learning difficulties and maintaining independence', in B. Bytheway, V. Bacigalupo, J. Bornat, J. Johnson and S. Spurr (eds) *Understanding Care, Welfare and Community. A Reader*, London: Routledge, 151–157.

Walmsley, J. and Ralph, S. (2002) 'The history of community care for people with learning diffficulties', in B. Bytheway, V. Bacigalupo, J. Bornat, J. Johnson and S. Spurr (eds) *Understanding Care, Welfare and Community. A Reader*, London: Routledge, 53–63.

Walsh, R. (1997) 'When having means losing. Music therapy with a young adolescent with a learning disability and emotional and behavioural difficulties', *British Journal of Music Therapy*, 11(1): 13–19.

Walsh Stewart, R. (2002) 'Combined efforts: increasing social-emotional communication with children with autistic spectrum disorder using psycho-dynamic music therapy and division TEACCH communication programme', in A. Davies and E. Richards (eds) *Music Therapy and Group Work*, London: Jessica Kingsley Publishers, 164–187.

Watson, T. (1998) 'Making connections – music therapy clinical work with people who have severe learning disabilities', unpublished MA thesis, University of Roehampton.

Watson, T. (2002) 'Music therapy with adults with learning disabilities', in L. Bunt and S. Hoskyns (eds) *The Handbook of Music Therapy*, London: Routledge, 97–114.

Watson, T. (2005) 'Fight, flight or work? Music therapy groups for adults with learning disabilities', paper presented at Music Therapy World Congress, Brisbane, July.

Watson, T. and Vickers, L. (2002) 'A music and art therapy group for people with learning disabilities', in A. Davies and E. Richards (eds) *Music Therapy and Groupwork. Sound Company*, London: Jessica Kingsley Publishers, 133–148.

Watson, T., Bragg, A. and Jeffcote, N. (2004) 'Working together – integrated multi-disciplinary practice with women', in N. Jeffcote and T. Watson (eds) *Working Therapeutically with Women in Secure Mental Health Settings*, London: Jessica Kingsley Publishers, 91–107.

Wheeler, B. (in press) *Music Therapy Research: Quantitative and Qualitative Perspectives*.

Whitehead, S. (1992) 'The social origins of normalisation', in H. Brown and H. Smith (eds) *Normalisation. A Reader for the Nineties*, London: Routledge.

Wigram, T. (1988) 'Music therapy – developments in mental handicap', *Psychology of Music*, 16(1): 42–51.

Wigram, T. (1989) 'Vibroacoustic therapy: the therapeutic effect of low frequency sound on specific physical disorders and disabilities', *British Journal of Music Therapy*, 3(3): 6.

Wigram, T. (1993a) 'Observational techniques in the analysis of both active and receptive music therapy with disturbed and self injurious clients', in M. Heal and T. Wigram *Music Therapy in Health and Education*, London: Jessica Kingsley Publishers.

Wigram, T. (1993b) 'The feeling of sound. The effect of music and low frequency sound in reducing anxiety and challenging behaviour in clients with learning difficulties', in H. Payne (ed.) *Handbook of Inquiry in the Arts Therapies. One River, Many Currents*, London: Jessica Kingsley Publishers.

Wigram, T. and De Backer, J. (eds) (2002) *Clinical Applications of Music Therapy in Developmental Disability, Paediatrics and Neurology*, London: Jessica Kingsley Publishers.

Wigram, T., Nygaard Pedersen, I. and Ole Bonde, L. (2002) *A Comprehensive Guide to Music Therapy*, London: Jessica Kingsley Publishers.

Williams, D. (1996) *Like Colour to the Blind*, New York: Times Books.

Williams, J. (2005) 'Achieving meaningful inclusion for people with profound and multiple learning disabilities', *Tizard Learning Disablity Review*, 10(1): 52–56.

Wilson, V. and Pirrie, A. (2000) *Multidisciplinary Teamworking Indicators of Good Practice*. Internet page at URL: http/www.scre.ac.uk/spotlight77.html (accessed 15/01/2005).

Wing, C. (1968) 'Music therapy in a hospital for subnormal adults', *British Journal of Music Therapy Newsletter*, London: British Society for Music Therapy, 8–11.

Wing, L. (1996) *The Autistic Spectrum*, London: Constable.

Winnicott, D.W. (1958) 'Primitive emotional development', in *Collected Papers*, London: Tavistock.

Winnicott, D.W. (1960) 'The theory of the parent infant relationship', in *The Maturational Processes and the Facilitating Environment*, London: Karnac.

Winnicott, D.W. (1971) *Playing and Reality*, London: Tavistock/Routledge.

Winnicott, D.W (1974) *Playing and Reality*, Harmondsworth: Penguin.

Wolfensberger, W. and Tullman, S. (2002) 'Community and stigma', in B. Bytheway, V. Bacigalupo, J. Bornat, J. Johnson and S. Spurr (eds) *Understanding Care, Welfare and Community. A Reader*, London: Routledge, 138–142.

Woodcock, J. (1987) 'Towards group analytic music therapy', *Journal of British Music Therapy*, 1(1): 16–21.

Woodcock, J. and Lawes, C. (1995) 'Music therapy and people with severe learning difficulties who exhibit self-injurious behaviour', in T. Wigram, B. Saperston and R. West (eds) *The Art and Science of Music Therapy: A Handbook*, London: Harwood, 288–295.

Woodward, A. (2004) 'Music therapy for autistic children and their families: a creative spectrum', *British Journal of Music Therapy*, 18(1): 8–14.

World Health Organization (1992) *The ICD-10 Classification of Mental and Behavioural Disorders: Clinical Descriptions and Diagnostic Guidelines*, Geneva: WHO.

Yalom, I. (1985) *The Theory and Practice of Group Psychotherapy*, 3rd edn, New York: Basic Books.

Zagelbaum, V.N. and Rubino, M.A. (1991) 'Combined dance/movement, art and music therapies with a developmentally delayed, psychiatric client in a day treatment setting', *The Arts in Psychotherapy*, 18: 139–148.

Zallik, S. (1987) 'In search of the face – an approach to mental handicap', *Journal of British Music Therapy*, 1(1): 13–15.

Index

abandonment 60, 62, 91
acceptance 37, 84, 87
accomplishments 80–2, 121
achievement 44, 45, 90
activity-based methods 37, 38
activity sessions 21
Adams, M. 16
adaptive behaviour 5
adolescents 36
adversities 29
advocacy 8, 9–10
aetiology 63, 73
affect attunement 27, 40, 102
affect regulation 61, 66
affective disorders 62
Age of Enlightenment 6
ageing 11
aggression 19, 31, 38, 62, 77
Agrotou, A. 51
alertness 45, 68
alienation 7
alienists 58–9
Alvarez, A. 35
Alvin, J. 13, 36
ambivalence 56, 60, 96
American Psychiatric Association 33
Amit, V. 85
anger 78, 93, 108
Ansdell, G. 14, 16
antenatal factors 6
Anthony, E. J. 30, 75, 79, 84
anticipation 54
antidepressant medication 68
anxiety 6, 29, 45, 61, 65, 69, 87, 93–4;
    considerable 78, 91; deeply held 96; effect of
    music on 14, 16; extreme 38; heightened 77;
    intense 68; maternal 34; significant disorders
    62; symptoms of 62; unbearable 26; see also
    separation anxiety
appreciation 94
arousal 41
art therapy groups 15, 89, 129–30
Arthur, A. 2, 13, 74, 118–19
ASD (autistic spectrum disorder) 6, 33–46
Asperger's syndrome 6, 34, 39, 62
aspirations 73
assault 18
assertiveness 55

assessment sessions 22, 23, 37, 42
asylums 7
Atkinson, C. 15
attachment 13, 46; fear of losing 61; positive 49;
    secure 61; severely compromised 60; strong 41
attachment theory 26, 50
attention seeking 53
attitudes 11, 90; defensive 87; medical and social 86;
    stereotyped 86
auditory sensitivity 42
authority 79
autism 1, 6, 15, 22, 98; modern day diagnoses 33;
    see also ASD
autistic-contiguous mode 44
autonomy 62
availability 30
avoidance 16, 40, 52
awareness 25, 26, 73; accurate 44; critical 50
Ayres, A. J. 37

Barnes, B. 75, 76
Barron, D. 7
Bates, R. 22
Bauman, Z. 85–6, 87
Bayley, M. 13, 72–3, 88, 96
behavioural approach 41, 49
behavioural difficulties 6
beliefs 11
Bell, D. M. 115, 119
belonging 13, 75, 84
benefits 8
bereavement 38, 55, 56, 117
Berger, D. S. 36, 41
Berrios, G. 58, 59
Bettelheim, B. 34
Better Services for the Mentally Handicapped (UK
    White Paper 1971) 73
biological factors 6, 60
Bion, W. R. 30–1, 40–1, 76, 103
bipolar affective disorder 6
Blackburn, R. 13
Boal, A. 89
body language 99, 102
body postures 49, 79
bonding 13
Bonnar, S. 91
Books without Words series 29
boredom 31, 96

boundaries 23–4, 39, 54, 55, 116; firm, within therapy 72; group 76; not impinged upon 122; personal 66; sexual 64
Bowlby, J. 26, 50, 61, 76, 90
brain deficiencies 34
Brechin, A. 86, 96
British Journal of Music Therapy 13
British Sign Language 10
Brown, H. 12, 32
Brown, S. 35–6
Brownell, M. D. 36
Bruscia, K. E. 37, 88
Bryan, A. 36
Bunt, L. 14, 28, 113, 120

care in the community 85; *see also* community care
care plans 42
Casement, P. 25
challenging behaviour 6, 16, 24, 47–57, 98, 115, 119
change 69; ability to manage 29; behavioural 62; clients reflect opportunities for 96; coping with 29, 38, 45; major 44; ordinary responses to 62; resistance to 33; therapeutic 55
Chesner, A. 15
childhood problems 62
choice 9, 25, 32, 80; denying 12; exercise of 13; making 37
circumstantial factors 48
citizenship 87
clapping 92, 106
Clarkson, G. 14, 37
class differences 72
clinical work 18–32
cliques 87
closeness 42, 49
Clough, J. 13
cognitive-behavioural approaches 49
cognitive impairments 34, 35
cognitive thought 16
Cohen-Cruz, J. 89
coherence 29; central 35; facilitating 29
cohesion 79
Coleman, S. 16, 18, 115, 116
collaborative working 121–32
commitment 55
communication 10, 13, 37, 75, 99–100; baffling 66; barriers to 93, 99, 102, 116; control and 114; developing 37; difficulties in 2, 6, 33, 34, 41, 60, 67, 72; early 38, 40; effective 118–19; effectiveness of using music to facilitate 35; efficient 9; emotional 36, 75; fluency in 104; ignoring 50; insufficient 69; mutual 49; non-verbal, person-centred 100; pre-verbal 36; rapid transformation of 52; regarding mutual clients 21; resistance to 108; social 114–15; two-way process of 35; unconscious 63
communication disorders 36
community 100; and culture 85–90; learning disability nurses 20
community care 51, 58
Community Care Act (UK 1990) 7
community presence 80, 82
competence 80, 81
complexity 69
compulsive behaviours 40, 41, 42
concern 66

condolence 26
confidence 29, 43, 44, 50, 92–3, 95, 96; building 27; diminished 20; need to develop 114
confidentiality 9, 21, 64, 101; not impinged upon 122
conflict 76, 95; disturbing 90; emotional 26; role 48; underlying 53
confusion 50
congruence 22
conscious 25, 35, 76
consent 20; informed 17
contact 20, 22, 43, 58; client's family 9; close 44; enjoyment of 41; fragility in 28; lost 67; need for 71; non-verbal, intense 49; positive 12; rhythmic and vocal 44
containment 27, 66, 76, 103; emotional 40–1; lack of 52
context 22, 63
continuity 29
control 96; and communication 114
Cooper, S.-A. 60
coping 38, 45, 91; discrimination and prejudice 91; greater skills 5; limited strategies 62
countertransference 25, 39, 46
Cowan, J. 13
creativity 36, 42, 58, 103
crying 66, 67
cues 5
culturally appropriate services 11
culture 20; community and 85–90; differences 72
culture-centred approaches 50
cutting 65
Cyprus 51

Dalal, F. 75
dancing 37, 43
dangerous actions 42
Darnley-Smith, R. 13, 15, 22, 122
Davies, A. 13, 30, 76
day centres 20, 77, 82, 90, 91, 96, 100
death 54, 95; child 64
De Backer, J. 36, 37
decision making 96; exclusion from 48
defences 26, 45, 108; psychological 26
deficits 2; adaptive behaviour 5; social functioning 5
deinstitutionalization 7, 85
denial 12
Denmark 7
dependence 31, 90; emotional 61
depression 6, 61, 62, 69, 118; psychometric measure for 117; recurring episodes 65; severe 77; significant factors in aetiology of 73; signs of 68
despair 49, 69
development period extract 43
developmental delay 15
developmental issues 60
developmental models 39
developmental stages 48, 60
diagnoses 6, 33, 37, 63, 65, 66; careful 62; different, implications of 69; difficulty in 69; lifelong 73; potentially far-reaching 60; psychiatric 59, 60; specific, varying 99
dialogue 68, 102; call and response 43; musical 46; reciprocal 40; turn-taking 40
difference 47, 87; exploration of 91, 94–5; gender, class and culture 72

Di Franco, G. 36
discrimination 11, 95; coping with 91
discussion 32, 92, 93, 107; group 53
disempowerment 53
distress 18, 19, 50, 53, 54, 63; articulations of 67;
    enormous levels of 42; factors potentially
    contributory to 60
DOH (UK Department of Health) 8, 10, 17, 47
Down's syndrome 6, 15
dramatherapy 15, 89
DSM-IV 33
duets 22, 44
Duffy, B. 116
Dury, Ian 112
dynamic administration 76

eating disorders 15
ECT (electro-convulsive therapy) 65
efficacy 16, 113, 117
egocentric tendency 41
Eisler, J. 121
Eliatamby, A. 9, 87
Emerson, E. 6, 12, 17, 48, 86
emotional difficulties 6, 74; controlling 77; largely
    neglected 2; recognizing and expressing 72
emotional health 12, 13; good, promotion of 10
emotional needs 14
emotional problems 13
emotions 2, 41; expression of 15; help to identify,
    understand and express 75; music is directly
    related to 36; negative, unwanted 27; shared 42;
    wide range expressed 43
employment 58, 74
empowerment 2, 10, 53, 96
endings 32, 96
endorphin production 48
energy 19, 31; creative 63
engagement 16, 106; musical and social 37;
    successful 22
England 74
enthusiasm 29
entitlement 58
environment 27, 39; auditory 43; optimum 28;
    supportive 32; use of 109
environmental factors 48, 62
envy 54, 96
epilepsy 6, 34, 48
Espie, C. A. 115, 119
Esquirol, E. 58
esteem 43, 44
ethnic communities 11
ethnicity 47
euphemism 7, 47
evaluation: joint 31; subjective 73
Evered, C. 90–1
excitement 64, 92
exclusion 7, 86
executive functioning 35
exhaustion 31
expectations 25, 55, 86; cultural 11; low 48
exploitation 62
exploration 50, 53–4, 93–4
expression: emotional 84; shared mode of 36
external realities 12–13
eye contact 40, 99, 106, 107, 126; sustained 43

facial expression 99, 102
facilitators 51, 52, 53
failure 90
fairy stories 15
family background 6
family history 62
family life 20
fear 29, 61, 99, 117
feelings 43, 60; acknowledgement of 49; deep and
    private 92; difficult 29, 41; discharged in broad
    gestures 61; envious 54; expression of 2, 15, 93;
    guilty 79; hard to interpret and verify 99; mixed
    93–4; negative 12, 32; out of control 22; positive
    29, 32; powerful 61; projected 27, 28; sad and
    happy 45; shared 2, 27, 44; strong 53, 55;
    therapist 21, 25; unacceptable 26; verbalized 46;
    ways to articulate thoughts and 30
Felce, D. 73
fight or flight 31
fighting 78
Firth, H. 72, 88
Fischer, R. 14
Fitton, P. 96, 100
flexibility 28, 89
Fonagy, P. 64
fools 6
Foulkes, S. H. 15, 30, 74, 75, 76, 79, 84
Foundation for People with Learning Disabilities
    29
fragile X syndrome 6
fragmentation 64
friendships 12, 71–84; extended networks 88
frustration 69, 77
fulfilment 12
Fuller, R. 116

Gale, C. P. 13, 14
gender differences 72
genetic factors 6, 34
gestures 61; meaningful 64
Glennie, Evelyn 95
global processing 35
Glyn, J. 30
goodbyes 96
Graham, J. 16–17, 38, 107, 108, 115, 116
Grandin, T. 37
Grant, R. E. 15
Gray, J. 85
grieving/grief 13, 26, 54, 60, 66
group conductors 75, 76
group therapy 30, 31, 71–84
Grove, N. 10

hair pulling 42
Hampton, K. 9, 87
Happe, F. 34–5
happiness 82
HAPs (health action plans) 10
Hartland-Rowe, L. 26
head banging 42, 48; repeated 76
Heal, M. 15
Heal-Hughes, M. 15
health 10–11, 20; better 117
health problems 6; frequent 99
Health Professions Council 121
health workers 9

hearing loss 6
hearing voices 65, 66
helplessness 73
Herman, J. 61
Hernandez-Halton, I. 25, 26, 27
Hewett, D. 102
Hills, B. 121
Hind, H. 15, 90
Hobson, P. 35
Hodges, S. 12
holding 27, 103
holistic approach 23, 101
Hollins, S. 18, 29, 90–1
Hooper, J. 14, 15, 16, 38, 41, 116, 128–9
hospitals 7, 13; process of closing 7; repeated admissions to 64
hostility 52, 99, 117
hugging 96
Human Rights Act (UK 1998) 8
hurtfulness 86
hypersensitivity 41

ideals 12
identity 72, 86; collective 74, 85; exploring 91
idiots/idiotism 58, 59
ignorance 86
illustrative records 20
imagination 33, 37
imitation 40, 46
Improving the Life Chances of Disabled People (UK 2005) 8
improvisation 15, 28, 36, 40, 43, 44, 45, 55, 63, 78, 80; free 22, 37; group 79, 106; interactions played out within 30; length of 44, 105; lively 79; temptation to keep short 107
improvisation assessment profiles 37
inadequacy 58
Include Us Too (publication) 12
inclusion 7, 8, 9; social 74, 84, 87
incontinence 47
independence 9, 10, 12, 13, 90; encouraging 2; exciting introduction to 11; promoting 89
inequalities 11
information 22; accessible 10, 20, 96; difficulty in processing 41; exchange of 9; musical and social 40; sensationalist and inaccurate 87; sharing 2, 128
inner disturbance 64
institutionalization 49, 51
institutions 87; long-stay, gradual closure of 73
instrumental playing 37
instruments 15, 25, 28, 33, 41, 43, 52; ability to play 96; arranging 23; behaviour towards 23; demonstrating 22; group members invited to choose 92; identified as a safe means of speaking and remembering 66; ignored or reflected offers of 68; larger 44; movements and positioning that might in using 101; opportunity to try 22; passing to and fro of 68; shared 40; small percussion 104; thrown 53, 54, 55, 108, 109
integrated approach 50
integration 69, 74, 87; aiding 100; real 88; social 13, 33, 37, 38, 58; *see also* sensory integration
intellectual functioning 98
intellectual impairment 5
intelligence 34

intensive interaction approach 49
interaction 37, 43; alternative means of 14; building skills in 37; client-therapist 15; difficulties 2; effectiveness of using music to facilitate 35; group 55, 78; infant-caregiver 35; intensive 102; intentional 106; interpersonal 34; mother-infant 15, 27, 36, 63; musical 27, 39–40, 92, 105; person-environment 5; played out within improvisations 30; positive 49; preverbal 39–40; sensitivity in 102; two-way, difficulties in engaging in 77
internal worlds 12–13
international research 17
intimacy 49; little opportunity for 61; psychic 102
involvement 56
IQ (intelligence quotient) 5, 77, 98
isolation 24, 38, 44, 74, 117

Jacobs, A. 122
Jay report (UK 1979) 7
John, D. 2
Jones, A. M. 91
Jones, P. 13, 16
judgement 47

Kanner, Leo 33, 34
karaoke 116
Kenny, C. 88
Kevan, F. 115
Kiernan, C. 17
kinship networks 88
knowledge sharing 114–15, 116–17, 117–18

labels 47–8; negative 7
Lacey, P. 98
Laing, R. D. 36
language 65; absence of 48; common 122; delay in 34; emotional 118; expressive and receptive, limited 16; hesitant and fragmented 66; inaccessible 29; understanding of 33, 34, 98
Lapper, Alison 112
Lapping, A. J. 75
laughter 92
Lawes, C. 16, 50
Leaning, B. 102
learning disabilities 1, 18–32, 58–70; definitions and causes 5–6; mild 2, 6, 16; mild-moderate 77; moderate 16, 20, 64; multiple 19, 28, 98–111; prevalence in South Asian communities 11; profound 15, 16, 19, 28, 50, 51, 98–111; severe 2, 6, 38, 75, 117
life events 29
lifelong learning 74
lifestyle: healthy 10–11; institutionalized 114; satisfaction with 73
limitation 27
Lindsay, B. 14
listening 54
liveliness 105
loss 13, 91; underlying experience of 70

McCarthy, J. 62
McCarthy, M. 17
McGill, P. 9
McIntosh, B. 87–8, 100

Macleod, F. J. 115
madness 59, 87
Makaton 10, 22, 29, 39, 91, 99
Mansell Report, The (UK 1993) 48
marginalization 2, 63, 84
mastery 29
Mattison, V. 32, 96
Mayo, M. 87
meaning 51, 99; potential 63; psychological 44; symbolic 49
meeting and greeting 96
memorizing facts 34
Mental Capacity Act (UK 2005) 8, 17
Mental Deficiency Act (UK 1913) 6
mental health 12, 13, 59, 69; dependent on community 75; good, promotion of 10; positive, developing and maintaining 29; service providers 9
mental health problems 1, 6, 99; acute 60
mental illness 58–70, 98
mental states 34, 64; fragmented 66; monitored 65; variable 66
'mentalizing' 64
mentally handicapped people 14
mind-reading ability 34
minds 34; development of 35
minority groups 11
Mir, G. 11
mirrors 40, 44, 68
Mitchell, A. R. K. 13
mood 105; management of 42; potential to escalate out of control 45
mood swings 77
morale 76
morality 6
mother-infant theories 27, 35, 61
motivation 72, 79
motor planning 41
mourning 13, 55
movement 41, 68, 102; music and 38
movement-based activities 37
moving on 96
multidisciplinary teams 9, 15, 37, 38, 41, 64, 66, 70, 121–32; assessments 23; close liaison with 42; file notes 21; music therapy as a diagnostic tool within 38; well-functioning 69
multiple causation 35
music 30, 63, 89; busy and disjointed 77; calm, gentle, repetitive 65; control of the structure of 66; discordant and disconnected 95; effectiveness of 35; fast and loud 93; fragmented 55; imaginative 29; intense 44; love of 38; moods and emotions expressed through 45; mutual making of 54; particular characteristics 28; pathological elements in 37; pre-composed 28; quieter 66; responsibility for sustaining 28; rich, harmonic 105; shared 43; soft, intermittent 104; spontaneous and communicative 27; taped 28; tightly structured 22; *see also* improvisation; instruments; pitch; rhythm; songs/singing
musical models 39

Nadirshaw, Z. 11
natural fools 6
negative behaviours 16
neurological damage 41

neuronal assembly formation 15
NHS (National Health Service) 7, 8, 10, 129
NIMBY (Not In My Back Yard) 87
Nind, M. 99, 102
noise 43
Nordoff, P. 35, 37
normalization 7, 14, 32, 73, 86, 88; drive for 12

O'Brien, J. 7, 80, 87, 88
obsessions 41; helping to cope with 42
obsessive behaviours 34, 62, 65
occupational therapists 41
O'Connor, H. 72
oddness 58, 64
Odell-Miller, H. 13, 30, 122
Ogden, T. H. 44
Oldfield, A. 16, 37
Oppenheim. A. N. 114
opportunist handicap 26
oppression 89
optimism 29
Our Health, Our Care, Our Say (UK White Paper 2006) 8
Ourvry, C. 13
outbursts 43; frenzied 66
outreach projects 20
Ouvry, C. 98
Ovretveit, J. 121

pain 31
pairing 31
panic 66
partnership working 118, 119
passivity 92
Patey, H. 13, 15, 22
Pavlicevic, M. 16
Pelham, G. 29
perception 73; internalized 26
percussion instruments 22, 40
perinatal factors 6
Perry, J. 73
perseveration 40
personality 10; musical 22
person-centred planning 8, 9–10, 100, 113
pessimistic assumptions 61
photographs 39, 93, 95
phrases 92
physical barriers 45
physical behaviour 37
physical delay 15
physical disabilities 6, 19, 101
physical illness 48
physical impairment 98
physical needs 22, 38
physical positioning 42
physiological functions 36
physiotherapists 41
pictorial timetables 39
Pistrang, N. 32, 96
pitch 36, 37; ability to imitate accurately 42
place 39
play 16, 27, 42, 46, 103; ability significantly impaired 33; imaginative, ability for 34; pop 'star' 43
playfulness 102
pleasure 22

PMLD (UK Profound and Multiple Learning
    Difficulties) Network 99
Porter, J. 99
positive behaviours 16
positive relationships 28, 42, 72, 73; aggressive 77
postnatal factors 6
power issues 56, 95
powerlessness 95
praise 79
predictability 34, 39
prefrontal capacity 35
pregnancy 6, 64; unwelcome 66
prejudice 86; coping with 91
preoccupation 67; primary maternal 61
preverbal adults 16, 19
Prichard, J. C. 59
Priestley, M. 25
Pritchard, M. 98–9
process notes 30
projections 66, 79; collective 87
projective identification 95
proprioceptive system 42
protection 21
psychiatric illness 34; treatable 62
psychiatric intervention 59
psychiatric wards 60
psychoanalysis 15, 24, 35, 50, 64, 75
psychodynamic orientations 37, 39, 63, 69, 76
psychogenic factors 34, 35
psychological factors 60
psychological illness 75
psychological needs 38
psychosis 61; behaviours associated with 62;
    indicators of 62
psychotic breakdowns 64
psychotropic medication 49
PTSD (post traumatic stress disorder) 62
public transport 116
pulse rate 14

quality of life 8, 14, 84; friendships and 71–4;
    relationships and 80–3

Race, D. G. 7, 9, 26, 87
randomized control trials 16, 50
Rapley, M. 72, 88
reality 27
reassurance 13, 76, 78
recognition 30
recorded music 14
re-enactment 50
referrals 18–21, 24, 50, 65, 67; more systematic
    reasons for 113; reasons for 22, 38
reflection 21, 23–4, 27–32, 42, 43, 44, 91; past
    negative experiences of 72; spontaneous 25
relatedness 52; creative 27; emotional 39
relating 50, 84
relationships 12, 13, 25, 30, 92–3; avoidance of 52;
    building 14, 27, 42, 79; developing 15, 36;
    difficulties with 77; emotional impact of 15;
    exploring 56; interactive 38; interpersonal 71;
    intimate 62; musical 49, 56, 64, 69; negative 72;
    opportunities for forming 2; parent-child 36;
    peer 72; possibility of 58; quality of life and
    80–3; reciprocal 100; reflecting 72; sexual 71;
    supportive 28; transference 72; trusting 38, 39,

54; turbulent 79; volatile 77, 79; working, useful
    23; see also positive relationships; therapeutic
    relationship
reliability 23
repetitive behaviours 33, 41; self-stimulatory 38
repression 12
resentment 78
residential services 8
resilience 30
resistance 33, 108
respect 80
responses 62, 67–8, 79; anxious 62; compulsive 43;
    conscious 35; emotional 38; improvised 64;
    responses musical 38, 42, 107; physical 38;
    traumatized 60; unconscious 35; verbal, to music
    92
responsibility 91
restraining devices 49
reverie 27, 103
Reyes-Simpson, E. 12
rhythm 36, 40, 41, 43, 92; simple recurring 68
Richards, E. 15, 30, 76, 90
rights 9
risk 76, 87; factors for mental illness 60; perceived
    52
Ritchie, F. 13, 14, 50, 51, 112, 114
ritual mourning 55
ritualistic behaviours 38, 42
rivalry 54
Robarts, J. 36
Robbins, C. 35, 37
rocking 108
role ambiguity 48
role models 72
roles 43, 48, 96; social 86
routines 33, 34; changes to 45
running away 47

sadness 56
safety 42, 45, 90
Same as You, The (Scottish Executive 2001) 9, 74
sameness 33
Samuel, J. 98–9
satire 112
satisfaction: lifestyle 73; pursuit of 71
Saul, B. 89, 117, 119
Saville, R. 89
scapegoats 79
Schalock, R, 73
schizophrenia 6, 62, 65, 66; symptoms 95
schools 9
Schutzman, M. 89
Scotland 74
screaming 42, 43
secondary handicap 15, 26–7, 50
secrecy 66
security 61; long-term 86; tangible means of 39
segregation 6, 74
self: coherent 64; contained, worthwhile 64;
    fragmented 64; integrated and coherent 70;
    rudiments of the experience of 44; true and false
    103; see also sense of self
self-advocacy 10
self-awareness 100
self-blame 74
self-confidence 79; lack of 72

self-damage 67
self-destructive impulses 65
self-esteem 13, 29; lack of 72; low 77
self-expression 37, 38, 49
self-harm 67, 68
self-image 77
self-injury 6, 16, 41, 42, 47, 50, 62, 67, 98;
    experiences underlying 68; gradually stopped 66;
    main emphasis on 48; prevalence of 49
self-protection 72
self-regulation 67; familiar 68
self-stimulation 48
sense of self 116; developing 45, 46; fragile 26;
    negative 26; understanding one's own 36
sensitivity 89, 98
sensory difficulties 42
sensory impairment 6, 48, 98
sensory integration 15, 36, 37, 38, 41
sensory sensitivity 34, 41
separation 61, 90, 91
separation anxiety 41
service planning 59
service provision 48–9; positive changes in 74
sexual initiation 64
sexual relationships 71
shaking hands 96
shame 58, 60, 64, 93
shared experiences 84, 85, 87
Sheehy, K. 99
Sheppard, N. 72
shock 60
shouting 66, 93, 107, 108
side effects 60, 63; potential 69
Signposts for Success (DOH publication) 8
signs 10
silence 28, 104, 109; poignant 43
Sinason, V. 6, 7, 24, 26, 31, 47, 50, 60, 99, 110, 115,
    117, 118
Skelly, A. 12
skin surface sensation 44
Smith, H. 12, 32
Sobey, K. 13, 28, 102
social change 89
social factors 60
social functioning 115–16; deficits in 5; difficulties
    in 60; extremely delayed 98; extremely delayed 98
social impairments 33
social interaction 85; difficulties with 34, 41; shared
    40
social model 8
social norms 60
social potential 116–17
social provision 59
social role valorization 7, 86
social services workers 9, 60
social skills 33, 38, 93, 116
social stories 36, 38
socialization 71
socio-emotional experience 36
songs/singing 39, 41, 43, 92, 93, 105, 107;
    commentary 40; familiar 28; modal, improvised
    52; pre-composed 13
sounds 38, 41; compelling power of 35; deafening
    44; dramatic 108; easily controlled 40; emotional
    qualities in 37; gentle 68; group 92;
    hypersensitivity to 41; interruptions from outside
104; low frequency 14, 16; musical 36; range of
    22; similar 49; using voice to create long lines of
    27; vocal 42, 55, 99
South Asian communities 11
South East London 113
space 40, 45; holding and thinking 69; long-term,
    protected 91
specialist services 48; psychiatric 60
specialized assessment criteria 60
speech 29, 33
spontaneity 30, 102
stability 45, 46, 76, 84
Stacy, J. 29
staff changes 45
stepfathers 65, 66
stereotyped behaviours 33, 34, 37, 65
Stern, D. 27, 40, 63, 102
Stewart, D. 27, 30
Stige, B. 88–9
stigma 6
stimuli 37, 38, 40; low response to 68
Stock Whitaker, D. 75
Stokes, J. 26
strange behaviours 62
stress 31, 49; potentially higher than ordinary
    factors 62
structure 37, 39
suicide 65
supervision 25, 26, 28, 30; constant 99; good 69;
    peer 31; regular 68; team 53
support 26, 29, 79, 88, 101; circles of 100; constant
    99; continuing need for 73; emotional 38, 45, 71,
    84; individual 8; social 71
surprise 30
survival 60, 71, 99
suspicion 52
symbolic interpretation 49
symbols 39, 50; accessible 10; see also Makaton
symptoms 62; immediate 70; painful 63; physical,
    behavioural alleviation of 14
Szymanski, L. 59, 60

tactile behaviour 37
talk 28; imaginative 29
teasing 58
teeth grinding 106, 107
television soap 93
tension 77, 78, 96
terminology 8
terms of abuse 47
texture 41
theory of mind 34
therapeutic alliance 23, 24
therapeutic intervention 2, 8, 123, 126; accessible
    100
therapeutic relationship 45, 50, 125; being in control
    in 114; conduct of 63; control in 114; formation
    of 39; long-term 65; positive and safe 45
threats 79
Thurman, S. 99
time 39
timing 40; exquisite 107
Tinbergens, N. & E. A. 34
Tizard, J. 7
Toigo, D. A. 37
togetherness 85

tolerance 54
Toolan, P. 16, 18, 115, 116
touch 41
Towell, D. 10
Townsend, B. 15
toys 33
training 9
transcription 16
transdisciplinary working 89
transference 25–6, 39, 46
transition 11, 38, 44, 45; ability to cope with and manage 29
transitional phenomena 103
trauma 61, 69; handicap as a defence against 26; profound 65; underlying experience of 70
Tredgold, A. 7
Trevarthen, C. 36, 63
triggers 42
true and false self 36
trust 46, 91, 92; fundamental problems in 61; mutual 76
turnover of staff 101
turn-taking 40, 44, 105
Tustin, F. 35
Twyford, K. 90
Tyler, H. M. 36

uncertainty 69
unconscious 25, 30–1, 35, 61, 75, 76; unpleasant realities denied and repressed into 12
unconscious observational learning 51
understanding 37; interpersonal 61; social 39
undressing in public 47
unhappiness 18
unreachable demands 48
Usher, J. 15

validation 96
values 12; collective 11; core 118; personal 11, 73
Valuing People (UK White Paper 2001) 3, 8, 9, 11, 49, 58, 74, 87
verbal abuse 64
verbal guidance 30
vibroacoustic therapy 14
Vickers, L. 15
Victorian era 6

Vinogradov, S. 31
violence 47, 64, 65
vision 6
vitality affects 102
vocal exchanges 68
vocal work 17; importance of 107
vocalisation 40, 38, 106; wordless 68
volatile behaviour 45
voluntary organizations 9
vulnerability 60, 61

Wager, K, M. 37
Walker, A. & C. 11
Walsh, R. 15
Warwick, A. 35
washing 41
Watson, T. 13, 15, 76, 90, 102, 117
Wechler Adult Intelligence Scale 5
welfare state 7
well-being 29, 73, 82; deterioration in 60; psychological 71
wheelchair users 19, 49
Wheeler, B. 16
Whitehead, S. 87
Whittaker, A. 87–8, 100
WHO (World Health Organization) International Classification of Diseases 5, 33
Wigram, T. 14, 15, 16, 36–7, 101
Williams, D. 9
Wing, C. 13
Wing, L. 33
Winnicott, D. W. 15, 27, 36, 76, 103, 109
withdrawal 38, 40, 62
Wolfensberger, W. 7, 12, 86
women: institutionalized 51; with mild and moderate disabilities 16
Woodcock, J. 16, 28, 50
Woodward, A. 36
words 29, 45; inability to express in 77
working through 65
working together 9, 100–1, 110, 130
worth 13

Yalom, I. 31, 71, 76, 84

Zallik, S. 13, 14